TWENTIETH-CENTURY CHORAL MUSIC:

An Annotated Bibliography of
Music Suitable for Use by
High School Choirs

second edition

by

J. PERRY WHITE

The Scarecrow Press, Inc.
Metuchen, N.J., & London
1990

British Library Cataloguing-in-Publication data available

Library of Congress Cataloging-in-Publication Data

White, J. Perry.
    Twentieth-century choral music : an annotated bibliography of
music suitable for use by high school choirs / by J. Perry White
-- 2nd ed.
        p.   cm.
    Includes index.
    ISBN 0-8108-2394-2
    1. Choruses--20th century--Bibliography. I. Title.
ML128.C48W53 1990
016.7825'026'4--dc20   90-20005

To Martha,

for her

Love - Intellect - Consistency

TABLE OF CONTENTS

Introduction to the First Edition   vii

Introduction to the Second Edition   x

SATB   1

SATB Divisi   110

SAB   145

SSA   154

TTBB   190

Music Publishers   200

Composer Index   205

Title Index   207

INTRODUCTION TO THE FIRST EDITION

Although fewer than twenty years remain in the twentieth century, the art music of the last eighty years remains relatively unknown to a large segment of the American society. Music of the seventeenth, eighteenth, and nineteenth centuries is still the preferred choice of a majority of the listening public. This is a troubling phenomenon in that the arts--particularly the visual arts and music--have traditionally been considered to be a reflection of and statement about the age and culture out of which they emerge.

Traditional music-education programs have contributed to this problem through curricula that do not give adequate attention to the literature and theoretical aspects of twentieth-century music. Because large numbers of teachers are relatively unfamiliar with both the literature and technical complexities of this music, they are unable to excite their students and encourage them in the understanding and appreciation of the art music of our time.

Practical and/or comprehensive bibliographies of twentieth-century choral music are rare, with most listings being of a very specialized nature (May, 1977; Klyce, 1968; Jessup, 1966). Walter Collins spoke of the need for systematic reference lists of choral music in his article "The Choral Conductor and the Musicologist":

> ...there have been only a handful of serious musicological efforts to provide systematic reference lists of choral music. Furthermore, those that do exist are not always designed to be of practical use to the performer. The list of Beethoven's choral music in Grove's Dictionary, for example, is very useful; but it is much less useful than Elliot Forbe's list, which includes information on performing editions, difficulty, cost, publishers, availability, and so on. Such lists are urgently needed in far greater numbers than they are presently being produced...[Collins, 1973, p. 126].

In preparing this bibliography the author has sought to survey a significant volume of twentieth-century choral music and to evaluate it according to its appropriateness for performance by high school ensembles of varying size, skill, and maturity. The annotations are intended to help guide the choral director to quality literature that lies within the capabilities of the high school student.

Music was selected for review through a systematic search of publishers' catalogues, the Kansas University Choral Library, other bibliographies, and the author's own personal library. An attempt was made to include all of the major figures of the century as well as those composers who initiated important trends during the period.

The bibliography consists of approximately 235 entries for SATB, SATB divisi,

SAB and SSA voices, and speech choruses. Works have been graded according to difficulty, and generally accepted ranges have been used in evaluating the appropriateness of the literature for high school voices. In some instances selections with rather extreme ranges are included, but this is indicated in the entry.

The bibliography is designed so that the music is categorized according to fourteen subject areas: composer, title, voicing, accompaniment, text, range, difficulty, style, publisher, price (when current), duration (when indicated), usage, publication date, and level. The criteria used in the selection of the literature are listed below.

1)   Ranges: The ranges of the voice parts are based on some generally accepted parameters for the high school singer. In most cases extreme tessituras are noted in the individual entries.

Soprano

Alto

Tenor

Bass

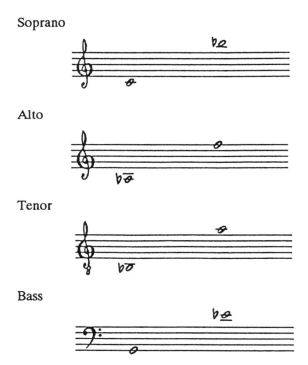

To indicate ranges in the bibliographical entries I have used the octave notation system recommended by the USA Standards Commission rather than including staff notation for each one. The octave notation system is shown below (Backus, 1977, pp. 134-135).

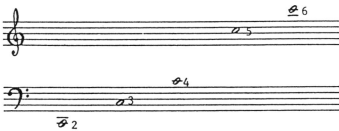

viii

2) Text: The texts are chosen from quality poetry and literature. An effort was made to exclude overly sentimental, trendy, or schmaltzy texts.

3) Difficulty: A subjective judgment was made concerning the average ability of the high school chorus; pieces were then classified as easy, medium easy, medium, medium difficult, or difficult. Pieces that were judged too demanding for the high school singer were excluded from the listing.

4) Accompaniment: The accompaniments are accessible to high school musicians. A variety of types is included.

5) Music: The music reflects a twentieth-century melodic, harmonic, and rhythmic language in an innovative and effective use of nontraditional chord progressions, added tones, dissonances, or other twentieth-century compositional techniques. The music chosen is structurally sound and enhances the text.

6) Usage: The selections are suited for use by a variety of types of high school choral organizations.

This work is published with the hope that these materials will guide both teachers and students to quality twentieth-century choral literature that is within the grasp of young singers. Because of the plethora of choral publications in today's musical market, it is often difficult to select music of lasting value that is suitable for young choirs. This volume is intended as a basic source book for the selection of such music, not an exhaustive study. It does provide, however, a good foundation for a continuing exploration of twentieth-century choral music. Choral directors who are familiar with the majority of these works will certainly be able to lead their students to a deeper understanding and appreciation of the art music of our time.

References _____

Backus, J. W. *The Acoustical Foundations of Music*, 2nd ed. New York: Norton, 1977.

Collins, Walter. "The Choral Conductor and the Musicologist." *Choral Conducting: A Symposium*, Eds. Harold Decker and Julius Herford. New York: Appleton-Century-Crofts, 1973.

Jessup, B. L. *Bibliography of the Choral Music of Daniel Pinkham*. American Choral Foundation Memo, No. 65, June 1966.

Klyce, Stephen. *A List of Twentieth Century Madrigals*. American Choral Foundation Memo, No. 76, February, 1968.

May, J. D. *Avant-Garde Choral Music: An Annotated Selected Bibliography*. Metuchen, N.J.: Scarecrow Press, 1977.

INTRODUCTION TO THE SECOND EDITION

With our entry into the final decade of the twentieth century, the concerns expressed in the Introduction to the First Edition of this bibliography some nine years ago seem even more pertinent today. Much of the art music of this century continues to be anathema to the contemporary student and the public at large.

Public school music programs have been subject to drastic reductions in both budget and programming due to fiscal constraints and curricular revisions. The music publishing industry, particularly those publishing houses that cater to secondary school music programs, seem to be increasingly driven by the popular trends of the marketplace rather than helping to encourage the production and sale of quality literature. Much of the interest in experimental, "avant-garde" music so prevalent in the 60's and 70's has now waned. In the public schools, the late 70's and 80's witnessed a blossoming of "show choirs" often at the expense of the previously popular madrigal group and chamber choir. There is now a plethora of tuneful, but intellectually sterile octavos flooding the marketplace, while music of real quality goes unsung.

I have attempted to include music in this volume that will help to fill the vacuum referred to above. In this second edition there has been an intentional approach to the inclusion of practical materials with the hope that directors will more quickly locate literature accessible to their groups. There is a broad variety of music included ranging from traditional sounding compositions to highly experimental works.

Reviewers of the first edition of this book encouraged a continuing update and review of new literature falling within the parameters outlined in the original volume. In response to that call, approximately 120 titles have been added, including more music for both SSA and TTBB voices. Particular attention has been given to selections published since 1980, but a number of older titles have been added as well. In those cases where music previously reviewed is now out of print, it has been indicated by an asterisk (*) following the title. These titles are still worthy of performance and have been retained in this volume.

In preparing the second edition I have utilized the *Prescribed Music List: 1987-90* published by The University of Texas (University Interscholastic League, 1987). This publication lists music for contests in that state and is among the finest and most comprehensive listings in the country. In addition, music was selected from the new prescribed list for the state of Oklahoma (Oklahoma Secondary Activities Association, 1989), and from complimentary review copies provided by numerous music publishers.

The criteria for music selection are listed in the introduction to the first edition

x

and remain the same with the exception that prices have been omitted because they change so rapidly. This bibliography is not intended as a comprehensive listing of twentieth-century choral literature for the high school chorus, but is offered as a guide to exciting and challenging materials appropriate for that group of young singers.

The first edition of this book was made possible by a grant from the General Research Fund at the University of Kansas, Lawrence. I am indebted to the University for its support of the original project, to Karen Andrews, who assisted me in reviewing literature for the first edition and to Ron Burk, who introduced me to computing at the University of Kansas. I wish to thank Vernon Davis for his assistance in preparing the second edition, and Boyd Fees of Fees' Sharp and Nichols Music Store for helping to locate publishers and additional literature. Finally, I wish to thank my wife, Martha, for her careful editing and proofreading of the manuscript.

References

Oklahoma Secondary School Activities Association, *Prescribed Band - Orchestra - Chorus Music List: 1989-92*. Oklahoma City, Oklahoma Secondary School Activities Association, 1989.

University Interscholastic League, *Prescribed Music List: 1987-90*. Austin: The University of Texas, 1987.

J. Perry White, Ph.D.
Director of Music
McFarlin Memorial United Methodist Church
Norman, OK 73070

Composer:	Adams, Leslie
Title:	Hosanna to the Son of David
Voicing:	SATB
Accomp:	Piano
Text:	Sacred
Range:	e4-ab5, Bb3-eb5, d3-g4, ab2-d4
Difficulty:	Diff

Style: Lively rhythmic anthem. Mid-section is in 7/8 and 5/4 meters contrasting with the 4/4 meter of the outer sections. Tonal but mildly dissonant with frequent added tones.

Comments: An effective setting of the text. Exciting piece for mature h.s. chorus.

Publisher:	Walton Music #2927
Usage:	Sacred-secular concert - Palm Sunday
Date:	1976
Level:	H.S. - college.

Composer:	Adler, Samuel
Title:	Some One
Voicing:	SATB
Accomp:	a cappella
Text:	Secular poem by Walter de la Mare - Someone came knocking at my wee, small door...
Range:	d4-a5, a3-c#4, e3-g#4, f2-c4
Difficulty:	MED

Style: Utilizes frequent parallel chords. Lively tempo with alternating meters. Added tones and passing tones result in mild dissonances. Dynamic coloration is quite important.

Comments: Good material for small ensembles. Requires strong soprano and tenor sections.

Publisher:	Associated Music Pub. Inc. A-266
Duration:	1:10
Usage:	Secular concert

SATB

Date: 1954
Level: H.S.

3

Composer: Ahrold, Frank
Title: The Bells
Voicing: SATB
Accomp: Piano
Text: Secular - Edgar Allan Poe
Range: d4-g5, d4-d5, d3-g4, d3-eb4
Difficulty: Med Easy

Style: Brisk tempo with driving rhythm throughout (quarter note = 170).
                     Extensive use of parallel chords. The part writing is conjunct. The
                     texture is primarily homophonic but is punctuated by short contrapuntal
                     sections.

Comments: An exciting work for young singers. This piece would work well for an
                     upper level junior high chorus as well as high school choir.

Publisher: Belwin Mills Publishing Corp. JF&B 9729-6
Duration: 1:18
Usage: Secular concert
Date: 1967
Level: H.S. - Jr. High

4

Composer: Archibeque, Charlene
Title: One May Morning
Voicing: SATB
Accomp: Piano
Text: Secular - English Folksong
Range: d4-d5, a3-a4, d3-f4, g2-d4
Difficulty: MED

Style: An arrangement of an English folksong. Each of the five verses is set
                     individually. The harmony is quite traditional with a few added and
                     passing tones. The melodic lines are conjunct. The texture is primarily
                     contrapuntal; the tempo and rhythmic movement are brisk.

Comments: A charming contemporary setting of an old English folksong.
                     Accessible to most high school choirs.

Publisher: National Music Publishers WHC Series #12

Usage: Secular concert
Date: 1969
Level: H.S.

5

Composer: Arnatt, Ronald
Title: Love Came Down at Christmas
Voicing: SATB
Accomp: a cappella
Text: Sacred - Christina G. Rosetti
Range: c4-f5, b4-c5, c3-f4, a2-c4
Difficulty: MED

Style: All three verses are set strophically, but the alleluia of the third verse adds a rhythmic variation and gives closure to the work. The verses are in 5/4, the alleluias in 6/4. Dissonant but accessible harmonies. Interesting voice leading in all parts.

Comments: A fresh, new setting of this familiar text.

Publisher: Boosey & Hawkes, Inc.
Duration: 1:45
Usage: Christmas
Date: 1989
Level: H.S.

6

Composer: Arnatt, Ronald
Title: A Spotless Rose
Voicing: SATB
Accomp: a cappella
Text: Sacred - Christmas
Range: d4-f5, a3-d#4, c#3-f#4, f2-c#4
Difficulty: MED

Style: Homophonic but with interesting voice leading in all parts. Rhythmic movement is in quarter and half notes and is smooth and flowing. Surprising dissonances and harmonic movement. A quiet and tender setting; the loudest dynamic marking is mf.

Comments: A lovely Christmas piece. Requires sustained and sensitive singing.

SATB

Publisher:	Boosey & Hawkes, Inc. - Oct B6466
Duration:	2:00
Usage:	Christmas
Date:	1988
Level:	H.S.

7

Composer:	Baksa, Robert
Title:	Walking So Early
Voicing:	SATB
Accomp:	a cappella
Text:	Secular - Sir Walter Scott
Range:	c4-e5, c4-c5, f3-e4, Bb2-B3
Difficulty:	Easy

Style: This is a simple but charming work, homophonic throughout. The meter alternates between 2/4 and 3/4. Rhythmic movement is in quarter notes in a moderately fast tempo; considerable use of hemiola gives further rhythmic interest to the piece. Mildly dissonant.

Comments: An excellent piece for a young high school or junior high chorus. The dissonances are mild, but give a distinctively contemporary sound to the piece. Good for developing blend and balance in an ensemble.

Publisher:	Tetra Music Corp. TC763
Duration:	1:40
Usage:	Secular Concert
Date:	1976
Level:	H.S. - Jr H.S.

8

Composer:	Baksa, Robert
Title:	Winter
Voicing:	SATB
Accomp:	a cappella
Text:	Secular from Shakespeare
Range:	f4-f5, c4-d5, g3-f4, c3-d4
Difficulty:	MED

Style: A rhythmic piece in 2/4 time to be sung in a light and buoyant manner. Both chordal and contrapuntal textures are utilized. Harmonies are mildly dissonant.

Comments: An interesting work that is rhythmically and harmonically attractive. A good piece for developing sensitivity to dynamic expression and the shaping of phrases.

Publisher: Tetra Music Corp   (Alexander Broude)
Duration: 1:30
Usage: Secular concert
Date: 1974
Level: H.S.

9

Composer: Barber, Samuel
Title: To Be Sung on the Water
Voicing: SATB
Accomp: a cappella
Text: Secular poem by Louise Bogan. Beautiful my delight, pass, as we pass the wave; pass, as the mottled night leaves what it cannot save.
Range: eb4-g5, Bb3-Bb4, eb,3-g4, ab2-eb4
Difficulty: Med Diff

Style: The piece is in paired duets throughout; the men's voices set up an ostinato figure depicting the motion of oars in the water while the primary melodic development is in the soprano and alto lines. Mildly dissonant. A great deal of rhythmic activity undergirds a sustained melodic line throughout the work.

Comments: A stunning piece. The sustained singing requires a mature choir. Careful tuning and support is critical.

Publisher: G. Schirmer   11644
Duration: 3:00
Usage: Secular concert
Date: 1969
Level: H.S. - college

10

Composer: Barber, Samuel
Title: Let Down the Bars, O Death
Voicing: SATB
Accomp: a cappella
Text: Secular poem by Emily Dickinson

SATB

Range:
Difficulty: MED

Style: Slow, sustained and dramatic. Alternation between major and minor
                      tonalities. Added tones, open fifths, and octaves characterize the
                      harmonic treatment. Dynamic coloration is essential.

Comments: The sustained singing requires a mature choir. Good for tuning,
                      phrasing and dynamic sensitivity.

Publisher: G. Schirmer
Usage: Secular concert
Date: 1942
Level: H.S. - college

                                        11

Composer: Barber, Samuel
Title: Anthony O Daly #2 from REINCARNATIONS
Voicing: SATB
Accomp: a cappella
Text: Secular poem by James Stephens - Since your limbs were laid out the
                      stars do not shine!
Range: c4-a5, a3-e5, c3-a4, g2-e4 Occasional high tessitura in tenor
Difficulty: Med Diff

Style: This is the second piece in a set of three. Moderate tempo in 3/4 meter
                      throughout. Contrapuntal. A drone or pedal tone runs throughout the
                      first 3/4 of the work, occurring first in the bass and finally in the
                      women's voices. Canonic techniques are used through most of the
                      piece. The repetitive style creates a dirge-like effect.

Comments: An exciting and intense work. Requires a mature h.s. choir.

Publisher: G. Schirmer, Inc.
Usage: Secular concert
Date: 1942
Level: H.S. - college

                                        12

Composer: Barber, Samuel
Title: The Coolin   #3 from REINCARNATIONS
Voicing: SATB

Accomp:	a cappella
Text:	Secular poem by James Stephens - Come with me under my coat, and we will drink our fill of the milk of the white goat.
Range:	d4-a5, g3-eb5, e3-gb4, f2-eb4
Difficulty:	Diff
Style:	Includes both contrapuntal and homophonic textures. Meter alternates between 12/8 and 9/8; movement is in a lilting rhythm. Mildly dissonant. Careful attention to phrasing and dynamics is required.
Comments:	An exciting work but should only be attempted by a very mature h.s. choir.
Publisher:	G. Schirmer, Inc. 8910
Usage:	Secular concert
Date:	1942
Level:	H.S. - college

13

Composer:	Bartók, Belá
Title:	Three Hungarian Folk Songs
Voicing:	SATB
Accomp:	Piano
Text:	Hungarian folk songs in English
Range:	c4-eb5, a3-a4, e3-d4, g2-c3
Difficulty:	Easy
Style:	Homophonic throughout. Modal, moderate tempi but in folk dance style. Triadic harmonies; little dissonance.
Comments:	Good material for young choirs.
Publisher:	Boosey & Hawkes
Usage:	Secular concert
Date:	1960
Level:	H.S. - Jr. High

14

Composer:	Bassett, Leslie
Title:	Collect
Voicing:	SATB
Accomp:	Electronic tape

SATB

Text:	Sacred - Almighty, Eternal, before whom nations fall
Range:	Bb3-g5, Bb3-d5, g3-ab4, d3-e4
Difficulty:	Diff

Style: Avant garde, aleatoric, pointillistic writing between voices. Some use of paired duets; mixture of homophonic and contrapuntal styles. Frequently changing meters.

Comments: Accessible only to very fine h.s. school choirs. A most effective and dramatic setting of text.

Publisher:	World Library Pub., Inc. C-2000-8
Usage:	Sacred-secular concert
Date:	1970
Level:	H.S. - college

15

Composer:	Bavicchi, John
Title:	Three American Choruses
Voicing:	SATB
Accomp:	Piano and optional brass
Text:	Patriotic - 1) Inscription on the Liberty Bell 2) Words of Igor Sikorsky 3) From an American pioneer monument
Range:	g4-g5, g3-d5, c3-f4, f2-d4
Difficulty:	Diff

Style: Mixture of contrapuntal and homophonic styles. Festive, fanfare settings. Quite chromatic and dissonant but cadences usually are triadic. 1) Brillante, quarter=92; 2) Sentito, quarter=66; 3) a la marcia, quarter=116.

Comments: Dissonant and difficult but interesting works. Good material for an adventurous chorus and brass group. Useful for patriotic occasions with fairly sophisticated audiences.

Publisher:	Oxford University Press
Usage:	Secular-patriotic concert
Date:	1978
Level:	H.S. - college

16

Composer:	Beadell, Robert

Title:	Sigh No More, Ladies *
Voicing:	SATB
Accomp:	a cappella
Text:	Secular text by Shakespeare
Range:	d4-g5, c4-e5, d3-a4, f2-d4
Difficulty:	MED

Style:

This piece opens in a lively 3/4 meter, then moves into a slower mid-section before returning to the original tempo. The outer sections are characterized by chordal writing and extensive use of 3rds. A lively and rhythmic setting.

Comments:

A well-structured piece providing an exciting setting of this familiar text. The high tessitura of the tenor line could pose a problem for young singers.

Publisher:	Canyon Press, Inc. 6503
Usage:	Secular concert
Date:	1965
Level:	H.S

17

Composer:	Beck, John Ness
Title:	A Hymn for Advent
Voicing:	SATB
Accomp:	Piano or organ
Text:	Sacred - Christ is coming, Christ has come
Range:	c4-f#5, a3-db5, c3-f4, g2-d4
Difficulty:	Easy

Style:

ABA form. Opening is in unison followed by mid-section in chordal style; after a brief instrumental interlude the original material returns. Extensive use of 4ths, 5ths, and added tones.

Comments:

A simple, well-written piece easily accessible to most h.s. groups. Good anthem material for the church youth choir.

Publisher:	Agape
Usage:	Sacred concert
Date:	1977
Level:	H.S.

An asterisk (*) following the title indicates that the selection is out of print.

18

Composer:	Beck, John Ness
Title:	Canticle of Praise
Voicing:	SATB
Accomp:	Organ or piano
Text:	Sacred
Range:	c4-g5(Bb5), ab3-e5, d3-g4(Ab4), g2-eb4
Difficulty:	MED

Style: This piece moves from a moderate tempo to a fast tempo, gaining momentum and intensity throughout. Homophonic. Utilizes rich, colorful chords (traditional and non-traditional). The accompaniment provides an exciting dimension to the work.

Comments: A beautiful, exciting piece creating a rich choral sound.

Publisher:	Theodore Presser Co.
Usage:	Sacred - secular concert
Date:	1964
Level:	H.S.

19

Composer:	Benjamin, Thomas
Title:	Sing and Dance
Voicing:	SATB
Accomp:	a cappella
Text:	Secular text by Kahlil Gibran - Sing and dance together and be joyful
Range:	b3-g5, g3-d5, e3-f#4, f#2-d4
Difficulty:	Med Dif

Style: Alternates between a driving, rhythmic section and a slower, more lyrical section, ending with an accelerando to the finale. Meter shifts between 5/4 and 4/4. Interesting part writing. Contrapuntal and imitative.

Comments: A good festive piece for the h.s. chorus.

Publisher:	Mark Foster MF 361
Usage:	Secular concert
Date:	1980
Level:	H.S.

20

Composer:	Berger, Jean
Title:	A Rose Touched by the Sun's Warm Rays
Voicing:	SATB
Accomp:	a cappella
Text:	Sacred - Pennsylvania Dutch text
Range:	e4-g5, a3-Bb4, c3-f4, g2-Bb3
Difficulty:	Easy

Style: Interesting combination of simultaneous duets between men's and women's voices. Chordal texture but voices maintain their individuality through the interesting voice leading. Added tones resolve to traditional harmonies.

Comments: A little classic. Good for small ensembles or full choir. Well within reach of most h.s. groups. Requires good low basses.

Publisher:	Augsburg Publishing House
Usage:	Sacred - secular
Date:	1962
Level:	H.S.

21

Composer:	Berger, Jean
Title:	The Eyes of All Wait Upon Thee
Voicing:	SATB
Accomp:	a cappella
Text:	Sacred - Psalm 145:15, 16
Range:	e4-f#5, f#3-b4, (b2)d3-f#4, (e2)g2-e4
Difficulty:	MED

Style: A legato work with long phrases. Primarily homophonic throughout. Frequently changing meters but tempo is quite slow so there are no rhythmic problems. Added tones create a lush, neo-romantic harmonic atmosphere.

Comments: A Berger classic, widely performed. Excellent program material, but not particularly easy because of the slow tempo and long, sustained phrases.

Publisher:	Augsburg Publishing House
Usage:	Sacred - secular concert
Date:	1959
Level:	H.S.

22

Composer:	Berger, Jean
Title:	Of Mirth and Merriment
Voicing:	SATB
Accomp:	a cappella
Text:	Secular - 1) Peanut Song, 2) Mirth and Merriment, 3) Help Yourself, 4) Four Farthings and a Thimble, 5) Betta Botta
Range:	c4-f#5, g3-d5, d3-g4, f2-e4
Difficulty:	Med Easy

Style: This is a collection of short, lighthearted, fun pieces. Most are set in a fairly quick tempo. Much tertian harmony is used. Mild dissonances.

Comments: Excellent pieces to include on a program for variety and for novelty numbers. Accessible to most h.s. choirs.

Publisher:	John Sheppard Music Press 2007
Usage:	Secular concert
Date:	1968
Level:	H.S.

23

Composer:	Berger, Jean
Title:	To Make a Prairie from THREE POEMS
Voicing:	SATB
Accomp:	Piano
Text:	Secular poem by Emily Dickinson
Range:	c4-g5, g3-a4, c3-f4, f2-d4
Difficulty:	Med Easy

Style: This piece is to be taken at a fairly slow, gentle pace. The meter is unchanging in 3/4. Homophonic. Mildly dissonant.

Comments: An attractive and accessible piece. Piano accompaniment is quite easy. Soprano solo.

Publisher:	Broude Bros. Ltd.
Duration:	2:15
Usage:	Secular concert
Date:	1973
Level:	H.S.

24

Composer:	Berger, Jean
Title:	I to the Hills Lift Up Mine Eyes
Voicing:	SATB
Accomp:	a cappella
Text:	Sacred - Psalm 121
Range:	d4-eb5, a3-a4, d3-d4, f2-a3
Difficulty:	Med Easy

Style: This piece moves gently in a moderate tempo. The writing is homophonic. Maj 7th chords occur frequently, but overall the harmonies are fairly traditional.

Comments: A well written, simple but attractive work. Well suited to the voices.

Publisher:	Augsburg Pub House 11-0678
Usage:	Sacred - secular concert
Date:	1978
Level:	H.S.

25

Composer:	Berger, Jean
Title:	There is a Garden in Her Face
Voicing:	SATB
Accomp:	a cappella
Text:	Secular text by Thomas Campion
Range:	c4-a5, g3-d5, d3-g4, f2-d4
Difficulty:	MED

Style: The piece moves gently in 4/4 time. A mixture of chordal and contrapuntal textures is used. Extensive use of dynamic changes. The harmonic treatment is mildly dissonant.

Comments: An expressive piece well suited to the voices. A good exercise in legato singing.

Publisher:	Broude Bros
Duration:	2:15
Usage:	Secular concert
Date:	1960
Level:	H.S.

Composer:	Berger, Jean
Title:	Proverbs #3 from AIRS AND ROUNDS
Voicing:	SATB
Accomp:	a cappella
Text:	Secular - Italian - Better a live ass than a dead savant
Range:	d4-eb5, d4-eb5, c3-d4, g2-d4
Difficulty:	Med Easy

Style: This piece is the third from a set of eight. It is a short novelty tune in a fast 4/4. Harmonies are traditional with some added tones producing mild dissonances.

Comments: A charming and effective piece, well suited to the voices. Good for variety on any program. Accessible to most h.s. choirs.

Publisher:	Broude Bros.
Usage:	Secular concert
Date:	1966
Level:	H.S.

Composer:	Biggs, John
Title:	Two Motets *
Voicing:	SATB
Accomp:	a cappella
Text:	Sacred - 1) O Lord spare thy people; 2) Praise ye the Lord, for He is good
Range:	e4-f#5, ab3-eb5, d3-g4, a2-d4
Difficulty:	Diff

Style: The first motet is quite short and moves directly into the 2nd without pause. #1 is slow with a plaintive motive that is introduced in all voices; tonal. #2 is faster, contrapuntal, and based on a 12-tone row. Short homophonic sections help to anchor pitch centers.

Comments: A difficult but rewarding work. Good for introducing music which does not adhere strictly to 12-tone formulas but is strongly influenced by them. Accessible to strong h.s. choirs.

Publisher:	Mark Foster CP-13
Duration:	3:00
Usage:	Sacred-secular concert

Date: 1959
Level: H.S. - college

28

Composer: Binkerd, Gordon
Title: O Sweet Jesu
Voicing: SATB
Accomp: a cappella
Text: Sacred - Lord Jesus, Thou art Sweetness to my Soul
Range: c4-g5, b3-d5, c3-g4, gb2-eb4
Difficulty: Med Diff

Style: A fairly lengthy, sectional, through-composed work characterized by
                     frequently changing meters and long melismatic passages. Tonal but
                     quite dissonant. Flowing legato style throughout in a moderate tempo.
                     Primarily contrapuntal.

Comments: This is a lengthy and difficult a cappella work. It is a fine piece, but
                     only an advanced h.s. chorus should attempt it.

Publisher: Boosey & Hawkes   5903
Usage: Sacred - secular concert
Date: 1974
Level: H.S. - college

29

Composer: Bliss, Arthur
Title: Sweet Day, So Cool
Voicing: SATB
Accomp: a cappella
Text: Secular - George Herbert
Range: eb4-eb5, b3-a4, f3-d4, a2-a3
Difficulty: Med Easy

Style: In a modified strophic form, the first three verses are set in a minor
                     key, and the last is in major. Homophonic throughout. Diatonic
                     harmonies with mild dissonances. Voice parts are primarily conjunct.
                     The work is in triple meter at a tempo of quarter note=96. There are
                     no rhythmic difficulties.

Comments: Good material for a chamber choir or a madrigal group. Would work well in developing good blend and balance. The text is a little heavy for young choirs.

Publisher: Novello & Co., Ltd. 29.0404 07
Usage: Secular - sacred concert
Date: 1967
Level: H.S.

30

Composer: Boyd, Jack
Title: Madman
Voicing: SATB
Accomp: a cappella
Text: Secular poem by Eleanor Wylie - Better to see your cheek grown hollow...
Range: c4-f5, c4-Bb4, c3-d4, g2-Bb3
Difficulty: Med Easy

Style: Mixture of contrapuntal and homophonic textures. Frequently changing meters. Moderate tempo, but quite rhythmic. Mildly dissonant, utilizing many added tones.

Comments: Accessible piece. Good concert material for developing choirs.

Publisher: Plymouth Music Co. Inc. PCS-33
Duration: 1:45
Usage: Secular concert
Date: 1964
Level: H.S.

31

Composer: Bright, Houston
Title: August Noon
Voicing: SATB
Accomp: a cappella
Text: Secular - adapted from "A Summer Ramble" by William Cullen Bryant
Range: Bb3-f5, Bb3-Bb4, eb3-f4, f2-c3
Difficulty: MED

Style: This piece is in a moderately slow tempo with frequent meter changes. Chordal and contrapuntal textures; legato. The harmonies are fairly traditional with some mild dissonances. Parallel 3rds are prevalent.

Comments: A tranquil work. Accessible to most h.s. choirs. Useful for developing legato singing.

Publisher: Shawnee Press, Inc.
Usage: Secular concert
Date: 1963
Level: H.S.

32

Composer: Britten, Benjamin
Title: Time from CHORAL DANCES FROM GLORIANA
Voicing: SATB
Accomp: a cappella
Text: Secular - Yes, he is Time, Lusty and blithe! Time is at his apogee!
Range: Bb3-a5, Bb3-e5, Bb2-g4, g2-c4
Difficulty: Diff

Style: Extremely rhythmic in a rapid tempo, the piece utilizes hemiola and other cross rhythms. Mildly dissonant. Basically an ABA form with brief coda; the central section is in duple meter, characterized by dotted eighth/sixteenth-note movement and contrasted with the faster triple meter of the outer sections.

Comments: The ranges are a little extreme for younger voices, but this is a delightful piece. It is quite challenging but within the grasp of a good high school chorus. A good work for developing strong rhythmic independence in the individual voice parts.

Publisher: Boosey & Hawkes (Set is 17411)
Usage: Secular concert
Date: 1954
Level: H.S. - college

33

Composer: Britten, Benjamin
Title: Time and Concord from CHORAL DANCES FROM GLORIANA
Voicing: SATB
Accomp: a cappella

SATB

Text:	Secular - From springs of bounty through this county streams abundant of thanks shall flow.
Range:	g4-a5, d4-e5, a3-g4, e3-e4
Difficulty:	Med Diff
Style:	In a rapid 6/8 time, the piece is written as a two-part canon with either the men's voices following the women's or vice versa. The paired duets alternate between tertian and quartal harmonies.
Comments:	Well within the grasp of a good high school choir, this piece would be a good introduction into some of the rhythmic and harmonic complexities of contemporary music.
Publisher:	Boosey & Hawkes (Set 17411)
Usage:	Secular concert
Date:	1954
Level:	H.S. - college

34

Composer:	Britten, Benjamin
Title:	Concord from CHORAL DANCES FROM GLORIANA
Voicing:	SATB
Accomp:	a cappella
Text:	Secular - Concord is here our days to bless, and this our land to endue with plenty
Range:	f4-f5, Bb3-c5, f3-f4, ab2-d4
Difficulty:	Med Easy
Style:	Homophonic. Slow tempo, through-composed. The work is tonal, centered around F maj.
Comments:	Readily accessible work for h.s. choir.
Publisher:	Boosey & Hawkes 5014
Usage:	Secular concert
Date:	1954
Level:	H.S. - college

Composer:	Butler, Eugene
Title:	Night Hymn *
Voicing:	SATB
Accomp:	Piano
Text:	Secular
Range:	c4-eb5(g5), g3-eb5, d3-f4, g2-eb4
Difficulty:	Med Easy

Style: Opens slowly and then moves to a faster middle section followed by a return to the original tempo. The meter remains constant throughout. Harmonies are traditional and fairly simple with some use of added tones. Basically homophonic.

Comments: An accessible work that is fairly simple but effective.

Publisher:	Carl Fischer, Inc.
Duration:	4:45
Usage:	Secular concert
Date:	1971
Level:	H.S.

Composer:	Butler, Eugene
Title:	Music Here
Voicing:	SATB
Accomp:	Piano
Text:	Secular text by Alfred Lord Tennyson
Range:	d4-g5, a3-c5, d3-e4, c3(g2)-c4
Difficulty:	Med Easy

Style: Piece is set in a moderate, freely moving tempo with occasionally changing meters. Fairly traditional harmonies with frequent added tones. A strong, rhythmic accompaniment complements the work.

Comments: An attractive work. Mildly dissonant; the added tones contribute to a lush chordal structure.

Publisher:	Carl Fischer, Inc.
Usage:	Secular concert
Date:	1974
Level:	H.S.

37

Composer:	Chavez, Carlos
Title:	Arbolucu, te sequeste *
Voicing:	SATB
Accomp:	a cappella
Text:	Secular - (English trans) Tree of sorrow, I bewail you
Range:	db4-g5, a3-c5, c3-g4, g2-d4
Difficulty:	Diff

Style: Melody is a Spanish folk melody. Many sharp dissonances, especially the use of the minor 2nd, resulting from a kind of pedal tone that pervades both the opening and closing of the work. In c min. Effective text painting.

Comments: An effective but difficult work. The triplet rhythms and melismas combine to create an almost agonizing mood in keeping with the spirit of the text. Requires a vocally mature group.

Publisher:	Mercury Music Co 352-00113
Usage:	Secular - sacred concert
Date:	1949
Level:	H.S. - college

38

Composer:	Clark, Rogie
Title:	Six Afro-American Carols
Voicing:	SATB
Accomp:	Piano (optional)
Text:	Sacred
Range:	b3-g5, a3-b4, d3-f4, g2-d4
Difficulty:	Med Easy

Style: Six carol settings. Traditional harmonies with occasional blues and gospel chords and progressions. Short homophonic settings of each text.

Comments: Appealing short pieces. Would make an interesting Christmas group.

Publisher:	Edward B. Marks
Usage:	Sacred - secular concert - Christmas
Date:	1971
Level:	H.S.

39

Composer:	Clausen, René
Title:	Set Me As A Seal from A NEW CREATION
Voicing:	SATB
Accomp:	a cappella
Text:	Sacred - Song of Solomon
Range:	c#4-d5, a3-g4, d3-d4, e2-d4
Difficulty:	MED

Style: Slow and sustained. The harmonies are basically consonant; suspensions and added tones create a harmonic tension enhancing the text. In ABA form; the A section is set homophonically, and the B section is contrapuntal with paired duets and limited use of imitation. Voice leading is primarily conjunct.

Comments: A beautiful work. There is limited divisi writing in the soprano, alto, and bass lines. The alto tessitura is a little low, and the work requires a mature bass section.

Publisher:	Fostco Music Press - MF 2050A
Usage:	Sacred - secular concert
Date:	1989
Level:	H.S.

40

Composer:	Clothier, Louitha
Title:	Lord of the Winds
Voicing:	SATB
Accomp:	a cappella
Text:	Sacred - Lord of the winds, I cry to thee. I that am dust...
Range:	g3-f5, g3-d5, e3-f#4, (e2)g2-d4
Difficulty:	MED

Style: Basically a homophonic texture. Changing meter but underlying pulse remains constant. Moderate tempo. Mildly dissonant. Movement in voices is primarily conjunct.

Comments: Effective setting of text. Good introduction to mildly dissonant 20th-century harmonies. Accessible to average and better h.s. choirs.

Publisher:	Greenwood Press
Usage:	Sacred-secular concert
Date:	1969

SATB

Level: H.S. - church

41

Composer:	Copland, Aaron
Title:	That's the Idea of Freedom from THE SECOND HURRICANE
Voicing:	SATB
Accomp:	Piano
Text:	Secular
Range:	d4-a5, d4-f5, d3-g4, d3-eb4
Difficulty:	Easy

Style: A patriotic work set in a marcato, march style. There is much unison singing. Harmonies feature frequent added tones creating rich chordal effects.

Comments: An effective work to use for patriotic occasions.

Publisher:	Summy-Birchard Pub. Co.
Usage:	Secular concert - Patriotic
Date:	1938
Level:	H.S.

42

Composer:	Copland, Aaron
Title:	Stomp Your Foot from THE TENDER LAND
Voicing:	SATB
Accomp:	Piano (four hands)
Text:	Secular
Range:	b3-a(b)5, a3-f5, b2-g(a)4, a2-e4
Difficulty:	Med Dif

Style: Work opens with solo bass voice; then men join and, finally, tutti chorus. A rhythmic, square-dance for voices. Central section features a soprano-alto soli duet answered by a tenor-bass soli duet, which then leads into a dialogue between the two groups. Typical Copland; mild dissonances, many open octaves and sixths.

Comments: An exciting, vigorous piece. Requires excellent pianists and a large chorus. Excellent festival music.

Publisher:	Boosey & Hawkes 5019
Usage:	Secular concert - Festival

Date: 1954
Level: H.S. - college

43

Composer: Dello Joio, Norman
Title: Sweet Sunny
Voicing: SATB
Accomp: Piano
Text: Secular. Lyrics by Barbara Anderson. Shine down sweet sunny, shine
             down on my soul.
Range: e4-e5, e4-e5, g3-e4, g3-e4
Difficulty: Med Easy

Style: In the style and spirit of a folksong. Short soprano and baritone solos.
             Homophonic. In a moderate cut time. Lowered 3rds and 7ths lend a
             slightly jazzy sound to the work.

Comments: Not a particularly distinguished work but good for the developing choir.

Publisher: Carl Fischer
Usage: Secular concert
Date: 1954
Level: H.S. - Jr. high

44

Composer: Dello Joio, Norman
Title: God Rest Ye Merry, Gentlemen
Voicing: SATB
Accomp: Piano - 4 hands
Text: Sacred - traditional carol
Range: e4-e5, b3-e5, e3-e4, b2-c4
Difficulty: Med Easy

Style: Homophonic. Is set in a stately, moderate 2/2 meter. Melody sometimes
             is set for soli voices or with humming accompaniment. The four-hand
             piano accompaniment provides good support for the voices.

Comments: An intriguing setting of a familiar carol. Interesting piano
             accompaniment.

Publisher: Edward B. Marks
Duration: 1:30

SATB

Usage: Christmmas
Date: 1971
Level: H.S.

45

Composer: Dello Joio, Norman
Title: The Holy Infant's Lullaby
Voicing: SATB
Accomp: Piano
Text: Sacred
Range: eb4-g5, Bb3-eb5, d3-eb4, Bb2-eb4
Difficulty: MED

Style: A smoothly flowing lullaby in 12/8 time. Mildly dissonant. Utilizes a mixture of homophonic and contrapuntal textures. Some use of paired duets. Brief unison passages. The melodic line is tossed back and forth between men's and women's voices.

Comments: A beautiful, sensitive choral piece. Excellent Christmas material.

Publisher: Edward B. Marks Music Corp. MC4240
Duration: 3:30
Usage: Sacred - secular concert - Christmas
Date: 1962
Level: H.S.

46

Composer: Dello Joio, Norman
Title: A Christmas Carol
Voicing: SATB
Accomp: Piano-4 hands
Text: Sacred poem by G.K. Chesterton - The Christ child lay on Mary's lap, his hair was like a light
Range: eb4-g5, c4-c5(f5), d3-f#4, c3-e4
Difficulty: MED

Style: In 6/8 time; the dotted quarter moves at 52 lending a lilting quality to the melodic line. Fairly traditional harmonies with some added tones. Homophonic with four-bar phrases throughout.

Comments: An interesting contemporary carol. Piano accompaniment is not difficult.

Publisher: Edward B. Marks
Duration: 4:00
Usage: Christmas
Date: 1962
Level: H.S.

47

Composer: Diemer, Emma Lou
Title: Three Madrigals
Voicing: SATB
Accomp: Piano
Text: Secular - Shakespeare
Range: c4-eb5, Bb3-d5, db3-d4, b2-d4
Difficulty: Easy

Style: #1 is lively in 6/8. Combines dialogues between men's and women's
                 voices with canonic treatment and short homophonic sections. #2 is
                 quite slow, homophonic, and has very close harmony. #3 is lively in 6/8,
                 similar to the style of #1. Mild dissonance and conjunct part writing.

Comments: May be performed separately but are best presented as a group.
                 Excellent pieces for h.s. choirs. Notes are easily mastered, but much can
                 be done with dynamics and phrasing.

Publisher: Boosey & Hawkes 5417
Usage: Secular concert
Date: 1962
Level: H.S.

48

Composer: Distler, Hugo
Title: Praise to the Lord, the Almighty
Voicing: SATB
Accomp: a cappella
Text: Sacred - Praise to the Lord, the Almighty, the King of Creation
Range: d4-e5, g3-c5, d3-e4, b2-e4
Difficulty: MED

Style: This is a setting of the familiar hymn, "Lobe den Herren." Primarily
                 contrapuntal with some use of paired duets. Mildly dissonant. The
                 work is highly rhythmic, utilizing frequent meter changes and dynamic
                 variations. Tempo marking is presto.

Comments: An exciting work that calls for careful attention to the individual vocal
                       lines. An accessible piece for a good high school choir.

Publisher: Arista Music Co. AE107
Usage: Sacred - secular concert
Date: 1966
Level: H.S.

49

Composer: Distler, Hugo
Title: Lo! How a Rose E'er Blooming
Voicing: SATB
Accomp: a cappella
Text: Sacred - Lo! How a Rose e'er blooming from tender stem hath sprung.
Range: b3-c#5, b3-a4, g#3-e4, b2-c4
Difficulty: MED

Style: In a chorale like style, but contrapuntal. Mildly dissonant. As is typical
                       of Distler, each line moves independently of the others in meter and
                       rhythm. The overall form of the piece is strophic in three verses.

Comments: A beautiful setting of the familiar chorale tune. Tuning and rhythmic
                       independence of each line is extremely important. Requires smooth,
                       sustained singing in all voices.

Publisher: Concordia Publishing House 98-1925
Usage: Sacred concert - Christmas
Date: 1967
Level: H.S. - college

50

Composer: Distler, Hugo
Title: Sing with Joy, Glad Voices Lift
Voicing: SATB
Accomp: a cappella
Text: Sacred
Range: d4-g5,(f)g3-d5, Bb2-f4, f2-d4
Difficulty: Diff

Style: An extended, sectional motet based on the early melody "Resonet in
                       laudibus." Rhythmic, featuring frequent rhythmic displacement, cross

accents, and polyrhythms. Extensive contrapuntal passages and melismatic writing.

Comments: A jubilant piece. Faster, more active sections contrast with the beautiful, slower and more sustained passages.

Publisher: Concordia Pub House
Usage: Sacred concert - Christmas
Date: 1973
Level: H.S. - college

51

Composer: Distler, Hugo
Title: Come, Spirit Divine
Voicing: SATB
Accomp: a cappella
Text: Sacred - German and English texts provided
Range: e4-f#5, b3-c#5, e3-f#4, a2-b3
Difficulty: MED

Style: Basically contrapuntal with interesting part writing. Harmonies are fairly traditional with mild dissonances; frequent use of 4ths and added tones. The closing section is homophonic. Occasional meter changes. Much attention to dynamics.

Comments: Requires skillful singing of the independent, contrapuntal lines.

Publisher: Joseph Boonin, Inc. B-292
Usage: Sacred - secular concert
Date: pub.
Level: H.S. - college

52

Composer: Distler, Hugo
Title: Lob auf die Musik
Voicing: SATB
Accomp: a cappella
Text: Secular - Praise to Music - German and English texts
Range: g4-g5, d4-d5, d3-g4, g2-c4
Difficulty: MED

SATB

Style: Work is set in a lilting 3/8 meter that alternates with slighter slower 4/4
                        measures. A mixture of homophonic and contrapuntal textures. Colorful,
                        mildly dissonant harmonies. Rhythmic with much use of hemiola.

Comments: Well written and well suited to the voices.

Publisher: Joseph Boonin, Inc. B 233
Duration: :45
Usage: Secular concert
Date: 1959
Level: H.S. - college

53

Composer: Distler, Hugo
Title: In the World there Is Pain
Voicing: SATB
Accomp: a cappella
Text: Sacred - In the world there is pain, but hear and be sure it will one day
                        be ended
Range: d4-g5, b3-b4, c3-f4, g2-c4
Difficulty: MED

Style: Frequent meter changes. The piece consists of two major sections, the
                        first of which is written in a moderately fast tempo and the second in a
                        slower adagio.   Contrapuntal and homophonic textures are used. Mildly
                        dissonant. Primarily conjunct part writing typical of Distler.

Comments: A beautiful, sensitively written piece with much room for expressive
                        interpretation. An excellent work for an average or better h.s. choir.

Publisher: Arista Music Co.
Usage: Sacred - secular concert
Date: 1971
Level: H.S. - college

54

Composer: Donahue, Robert
Title: On Christmas Day
Voicing: SATB
Accomp: a cappella
Text: Sacred - In the quiet of the night we wait for him
Range: d4-f5, Bb3- c5, d3-d4, d3-a3

Difficulty:	Easy
Style:	ABA form. Individual entries and duets alternating with homophonic texture. Very mild dissonances yet has a distinctively contemporary sound. Changing meters and triplet rhythms; tempo is moderate.
Comments:	An accessible piece for young h.s. singers. Good for acquainting the ear with sharp dissonances.
Publisher:	World Library Pub., Inc. 7624-8
Usage:	Christmas
Date:	1980
Level:	H.S.

55

Composer:	Durufle, Maurice
Title:	Tantum ergo from QUATRE MOTETS
Voicing:	SATB
Accomp:	a cappella
Text:	Sacred - Latin
Range:	d4-f5, g3-c5, d3-g4, g2-d4
Difficulty:	MED
Style:	Contrapuntal and chantlike with frequently changing meter to maintain the syllabic accent of the text. Lush harmonies and frequent suspension-resolution figures.
Comments:	Of the 4 motets, the "Ubi caritas" is certainly the most stunning, but this too is a very beautiful setting. Requires a mature choir to effectively carry the interior phrasing of the work.
Publisher:	Durand & Cie
Usage:	Sacred-secular concert
Date:	1960
Level:	H.S. - college

56

Composer:	Durufle, Maurice
Title:	Tu es Petrus #3 of QUATRE MOTETS
Voicing:	SATB
Accomp:	a cappella
Text:	Sacred - Latin

SATB

Range:	a4-a5, d4-c5, f#3-g4, b2-d4
Difficulty:	MED

Style: Contrapuntal. Frequently changing meter used to maintain a chantlike melodic movement. Mild dissonances and lush harmonies typical of Durufle's writing.

Comments: A short, but lovely motet setting. Accessible to the average or better h.s. choir.

Publisher:	Durand & Cie
Usage:	Sacred-secular concert
Date:	1960
Level:	H.S. - college

57

Composer:	Duson, Dede
Title:	The Elusive Quest
Voicing:	SATB
Accomp:	Piano, oboe
Text:	Secular - Gwen Frostic - Follow the elusive quest for what the mind can perceive...
Range:	c#4-g5, c#4-c#5, e3-g4, c3-d4
Difficulty:	Med Easy

Style: The texture of the work is homophonic throughout. The oboe introduces a melodic motive that recurs throughout the work. There are numerous sixteenth-note figurations, but at the suggested tempo [quarter note=48] they are not problematic. Tertian harmonies. The oboe nicely complements the vocal lines and is used in alternation with them.

Comments: This piece would work well with a young high school chorus and is readily accessible to them.

Publisher:	Neil A. Kjos Music Co. Ed. 8687
Usage:	Secular concert - Commencement
Date:	1988
Level:	H.S.

58

Composer:	Effinger, Cecil
Title:	If You Your Lips Would Keep from Slips *
Voicing:	SATB
Accomp:	a cappella
Text:	Secular
Range:	c4-g5, g3-d5, c3-f#4, f2-c4
Difficulty:	MED

Style: This piece is a contemporary madrigal. It is mildly dissonant with frequent use of parallel 3rds. Primarily homophonic. Meter alternates between 4/4 and 3/4.

Comments: An effective, fun piece. Would be a good, lighthearted addition to the concert program.

Publisher:	G. Schirmer 11769
Usage:	Secular concert
Date:	1971
Level:	H.S. - college

59

Composer:	Effinger, Cecil
Title:	By the Springs of Water
Voicing:	SATB
Accomp:	Organ or piano
Text:	Sacred - Isaiah 49:10
Range:	c4-g5, c4-d5, c3-f#4, f2-d4
Difficulty:	MED

Style: Basically homophonic, supported by a simple but effective accompaniment. Outer sections are fairly slow and calm, contrasting with a faster, more rhythmic mid-section. Frequent meter changes. Contemporary harmonies but only mildly dissonant; tonal.

Comments: Requires a fairly large and aggressive chorus. An interesting and exciting work.

Publisher:	Augsburg Publishing House
Usage:	Sacred - secular concert
Date:	1975
Level:	H.S.

60

Composer:	Effinger, Cecil
Title:	Basket #3 of FOUR PASTORALES
Voicing:	SATB
Accomp:	Solo oboe
Text:	Secular - Know me then. The children out of the shade have brought me a basket.
Range:	c4-eb5, Bb3-Bb4, c3-eb4, f2-c4
Difficulty:	MED

Style: ABA form; homophonic; some use of bitonality. Opens in a moderate 9/8 movement. Central section is in 4/4. Frequently shifting meter and juxtaposition of duplet and triplet figurations.

Comments: Probably the most difficult of the set, but still accessible to the average h.s. chorus.

Publisher:	G. Schirmer Inc. 11061
Duration:	2:30
Usage:	Secular concert
Date:	1964
Level:	H.S. - college

61

Composer:	Effinger, Cecil
Title:	Wood #4 from FOUR PASTORALES
Voicing:	SATB
Accomp:	Solo oboe
Text:	Secular - There was a dark and awful wood where increments of death accrued to every leaf and antlered head
Range:	d4-g5, Bb3-eb5, d3-f#4, Bb2-eb4
Difficulty:	MED

Style: Homophonic. Unison sections set off more dissonant chordal sections. Effective text painting. Opening section marked risoluto, then moves to agitato and finally concludes with a broad, stately finale. Conjunct movement in parts.

Comments: Set should be in the h.s. repertoire. Fine, accessible material.

Publisher:	G. Schirmer 11062
Duration:	3:30

Usage: Secular concert
Date: 1964
Level: H.S. - college

62

Composer: Effinger, Cecil
Title: Noon #2 from FOUR PASTORALES
Voicing: SATB
Accomp: Solo oboe
Text: Secular - Noon is half the passion of light...
Range: eb4-d5, cb4-c5, c3-e4, a2-c4
Difficulty: Med Easy

Style: Much use of paired duets moving chromatically in 3rds. Some use of bitonality. Slow, pensive (lazy) mood; very descriptive of text. Basic movement is in quarter and half notes.

Comments: Accessible and effective work. These works can be done either individually or as a set. The oboe accompaniment provides an interesting change of timbre in building a program.

Publisher: G. Schirmer 11060
Duration: 3:30
Usage: Secular concert
Date: 1964
Level: H.S. - college

63

Composer: Effinger, Cecil
Title: No Mark #1 from FOUR PASTORALES
Voicing: SATB
Accomp: Solo oboe
Text: Secular - Corn grew where the corn was spilled in the wreck where Casey Jones was killed
Range: c4-db5, gb3-d5, d3-d4, Bb2-d4
Difficulty: Med Easy

Style: Short martial phrases in a moderate allegro. Closes with a slower plaintive treatment. Homophonic; tonal; mild dissonances. Primarily quarter note movement.

Comments: Singable piece for high school groups. The set is now a standard part of the literature.

Publisher: G. Schirmer Inc.
Duration: 2:30
Usage: Secular concert
Date: 1964
Level: H.S.- college

64

Composer: Felciano, Richard
Title: Rocking *
Voicing: SATB
Accomp: a cappella
Text: Czech carol - Little Jesus, sweetly sleep
Range: c4-d5, c4-a4, e3-d4, (F2)b2-c4
Difficulty: Easy

Style: A traditional setting of this familiar carol, but tastefully done. An easy but intriguing and appealing arrangement. Mixture of homophonic and contrapuntal writing. Male voices establish a gentle rocking rhythm in middle section.

Comments: Good Christmas material for the young choir.

Publisher: Edward B. Marks
Duration: 1:10
Usage: Christmas
Date: 1970
Level: H.S. - Jr. High

65

Composer: Felciano, Richard
Title: The Eyes of All Hope in Thee, O Lord
Voicing: SATB
Accomp: a cappella
Text: Sacred - Psalms 144 and 167
Range: f4-f#5, db4-b4, f3-e4, a2-c4

Difficulty:	MED
Style:	The work is primarily contrapuntal with short homophonic statements. Sectional, although the second half of the piece is built around an alleluia that appears in all four voices in semi-fugal style. Mild dissonances. Moderate tempo; flowing eighth-note rhythm and some sixteenth-note figures.
Comments:	An accessible motet for the h.s. choir. The ranges are comfortable for the voices. Flowing, conjunct melody.
Publisher:	E. C. Schirmer - ECS No. 2918
Usage:	Sacred concert
Date:	1973
Level:	H.S.

66

Composer:	Fetler, Paul
Title:	Wild Swans
Voicing:	SATB
Accomp:	a cappella
Text:	Secular poem by Edna St. Vincent Millay
Range:	d4-g5, a3-d5, d3-e4, g2-c4 Sustained high g in soprano
Difficulty:	Med Diff
Style:	Alternates between contrapuntal and homophonic textures. Chromatic writing results in sharp dissonances. Moderage tempo. Part-writing is mostly conjunct. Haunting melody; interesting use of pedal tones in bass.
Comments:	Good contest material for the adventurous director. Requires attention to phrasing. Deserves performance.
Publisher:	Associated Music Pub. A-245
Duration:	1:52
Usage:	Secular concert
Date:	1957
Level:	H.S. - college

67

Composer:	Fetler, Paul
Title:	All Day I Hear

Voicing:	SATB
Accomp:	a cappella
Text:	Secular poem by James Joyce - All day I Hear the noise of waters making moan.
Range:	e4-g5, a3-d5, e3-d4, g2-c4
Difficulty:	Med Diff
Style:	Primarily homophonic. Conjunct voice leading for the most part. 2nds and 7ths are prevalent in the harmony; many added tones are used. Plaintive melody; moderately slow tempo.
Comments:	Requires a fairly mature choir. Long, sustained phrases. A lovely work, worthy of performance.
Publisher:	Lawson-Gould 682
Usage:	Secular concert
Date:	1957
Level:	H.S.

68

Composer:	Fetler, Paul
Title:	Hosanna *
Voicing:	SATB
Accomp:	Piano or organ
Text:	Sacred - Hosanna to the living Lord
Range:	c4-g5, (g)a3-eb5, c3-g4, g2-eb4 Ten & bass tessituras a little high.
Difficulty:	Med Easy
Style:	This is a lively piece in 3/4 with quarter note=132. Rhythmic with extensive use of syncopation. Percussive accompaniment. Repetition of a basic rhythmic figure occurs throughout the piece. Modal.
Comments:	A good festive work. Good concert material.
Publisher:	Augsburg Pub House 11-1647
Usage:	Sacred - secular concert
Date:	1971
Level:	H.S.

69

Composer:	Fink, Michael
Title:	What Sweeter Music

Voicing:	SATB
Accomp:	Triangle, guitar and piano or harp
Text:	Sacred - Robert Herrick - What sweeter music can we bring than a carol for to sing.
Range:	e4-d5, d4-b5, e3-g#4, g2-e4
Difficulty:	MED

Style: The vocal texture is homophonic juxtaposed with an interesting instrumental accompaniment that complements the text. Very rhythmic. The piece is in ABA form; the beginning and short ending are in a somewhat pastorale style while the large central section is set in fanfare style. There is a great deal of parallel movement utilizing traditional chordal structures.

Comments: A wonderful piece for Christmas or for general use. The guitar-harp accompaniment provides a marvelous variation from typical piano accompaniments.

Publisher:	E.C. Schirmer 2771
Usage:	Christmas concert
Date:	1970
Level:	H.S.-College-Church

70

Composer:	Fink, Michael
Title:	Full Fadom Five Thy Father Lies (second setting)
Voicing:	SATB
Accomp:	a cappella
Text:	Secular text by Shakespeare
Range:	d4-eb5, a3-Bb4, d3-f4, g2-c4
Difficulty:	MED

Style: This piece is set in a moderate tempo with frequently changing meters in the opening section. The opening section utilizes colorful, mildly dissonant, chordal writing. The last section is rhythmically more subdued. A pedal tone occurs in the bass line. Interesting special effects are utilized in the closing section.

Comments: An effective work. Interesting program material.

Publisher:	Mark Foster Music Co. MF344D
Usage:	Secular concert
Date:	
Level:	H.S.

71

Composer:	Fissinger, Edwin
Title:	Psalm 117 *
Voicing:	SATB
Accomp:	a cappella
Text:	Sacred - Psalm 117 - O Praise the Lord all ye nations
Range:	d#4-g#5, b3-d5, d#3-f#4, b2-d#4
Difficulty:	MED

Style:	Opens with an imitative exclamation in all 4 voices. Highly rhythmic with quartal harmonies; frequent use of major and minor 2nds. Through-composed but has a contrasting, slow middle section.
Comments:	A good joyful anthem for concert use. In a fanfare style. Accessible for average or better h.s. choirs.

Publisher:	World Library of Sacred Music
Usage:	Sacred-secular concert
Date:	1961
Level:	H.S. - college

72

Composer:	Frackenpohl, Arthur
Title:	Never Doubt I Love
Voicing:	SATB
Accomp:	a cappella
Text:	Secular - Shakespeare
Range:	d4-a5, Bb3-c5, d3-f#4, g2-c#4
Difficulty:	Med Easy

Style:	An expressive part-song. In a moderate 3/4, the work is homophonic throughout. Much use of added tones and tertian harmonies. Mildly dissonant. No rhythmic problems. A smooth, legato style is used throughout the work.
Comments:	Good material for the madrigal group or chamber choir. Accessible but solid material. Soprano solo.

Publisher:	Piedmont Music Co., Inc. MC4285
Duration:	2:40

Usage: Secular concert
Date: 1964
Level: H.S.

73

Composer: Frackenpohl, Arthur
Title: Lovers Love the Spring
Voicing: SATB
Accomp: Piano
Text: Secular - Shakespeare. It was a lover and his lass
Range: e4-g5, b3-c5, g3-f4, c3-c4
Difficulty: Easy

Style: Homophonic. Quite rhythmic with frequent syncopation. ABA form. In mid-section melody is tossed between voices. Playful, novelty number. Features frequent open fifths.

Comments: A good, fun tune for young choirs.

Publisher: Edward B. Marks
Duration: 1:05
Usage: Secular concert
Date: 1960
Level: H.S. - jr. high

74

Composer: Gardner, John
Title: Tomorrow Shall Be My Dancing Day
Voicing: SATB
Accomp: Piano, tambourine, side drum
Text: Traditional sacred
Range: a3-g5, a3-e5, d3-g4, g2-e4
Difficulty: MED

Style: This setting is rhythmic with changing meters throughout. The piano accompaniment accentuates cross accents which occur frequently in the vocal line. Dissonances result from generous utilization of added tones and passing tones. The use of tambourine and side drum make this an especially refreshing and exciting piece.

Comments: Rhythmically challenging; the melodic and harmonic writing is singable, making this a rewarding piece for a good high school chorus.

Publisher: Oxford University Press   40.107
Usage: Sacred-secular concert
Date: 1966
Level: H.S.-church youth

75

Composer: Goemanne, Noel
Title: Clap Your Hands
Voicing: SATB
Accomp: Piano
Text: Sacred - Psalms
Range: c4-g5, c4-b4, f#3-d4, c3-c4
Difficulty: MED

Style: Rhythmic with shifting meters. Oscillates between major and minor modes. Frequent open fifths and parallel chords. The accompaniment is quite complex and rhythmic.

Comments: An exciting piece that is accessible to younger choirs. Rhythmic figures are announced and then repeated. Voice ranges are restricted. Good program music.

Publisher: Shawnee Press, Inc. A-1838
Duration: 3:00
Usage: Sacred-secular concert
Date: 1988
Level: H.S. - Jr. High

76

Composer: Gooch, Warren P.
Title: Very Long Ago
Voicing: SATB
Accomp: Piano, string or electric bass
Text: Sacred
Range: a3-f5, a3-f5, a2-f4, a2-f4
Difficulty: MED

Style: This piece is characterized by an ostinato figure in 7/8 meter that permeates the entire work. A recurring chorus is set in 6/8 meter and provides relief from and contrast with the 7/8 ostinato figure. The formal structure is a modified strophic consruction. Quartal harmonies are used, which combined with the 7/8 meter, lend the work a distinctively native American character.

Comments: An interesting work. Not particularly difficult after the 7/8 meter is mastered. Good material for a church youth choir.

Publisher: Augsburg Publishing House
Usage: Sacred concert - Eastertide
Date: 1987
Level: H.S.

77

Composer: Grantham, Donald
Title: This Is My Letter to the World from SEVEN CHORAL SETTINGS OF POEMS BY EMILY DICKINSON
Voicing: SATB
Accomp: A cappella
Text: Secular
Range: c#4-E5, g3-b4, c#3-d4, e#2-c#4
Difficulty: Med Diff

Style: A quiet, pastoral setting characterized by mild dissonances. The texture is a mixture of contrapuntal and homophonic styles. Occasional sharp dissonances result from melodic movement in the individual voice parts.

Comments: A difficult piece for high school singers, but if the vocal lines are learned melodically, the dissonances will not be problematic. The bass line requires a strong second bass section. A beautiful piece.

Publisher: E.C. Schirmer 3072
Usage: Secular concert
Date: 1983
Level: H.S. - College

78

Composer: Gustafson, Dwight
Title: Three Songs of Parting *
Voicing: SATB
Accomp: Piano
Text: Secular poems by Walt Whitman -1) Joy, Shipmate, Joy!; 2) The Dismantled Ship; 3) Now Finale to the Shore
Range: d4-a5, g3-c#5, d3-f#4, (e)f2-d4

SATB

Difficulty:	MED
Style:	#1 is in a fast tempo, #2 in a slow tempo and #3 in a moderate tempo. The middle piece is quiet and legato and contrasts with the more maestoso outer movements. The works are basically homophonic. Contemporary, tonal harmonies; mildly dissonant. Piano accompaniment is not difficult but effectively complements the voices.
Comments:	An excellent set, well suited to the voices. Fine program material.
Publisher:	Shawnee Press, Inc. A-897
Duration:	6:00
Usage:	Secular concert
Date:	1967
Level:	H.S.

79

Composer:	Hageman, Philip
Title:	Eldorado
Voicing:	SATB
Accomp:	Piano
Text:	Secular - Edgar Allan Poe
Range:	a3-g5, f#3-f#5, eb3-ab4, c3-f#4
Difficulty:	Med Dif
Style:	The work is in 6/8 meter throughout; the accompaniment introduces a triplet figure that creates the imagery of a galloping horse. The vocal parts move primarily in dotted quarter figures, frequently punctuated with quarter-note duplets against the accompaniment. Quite dissonant, but the dissonances are generally approached through consonant harmonies. Melodic lines are disjunct; the texture is primarily homophonic with short imitative exclamations at cadence points.
Comments:	Even though the ranges in the inner parts are extreme, the tessitura of each voice is good. A challenging but satisfying work for a mature high school choir. The poem deals with the search for Eldorado, a mythical place of fabulous riches.
Publisher:	Oxford University Press 95.212
Duration:	4:00
Usage:	Secular concert
Date:	1987
Level:	H.S. - College

80

Composer:	Harris, Robert A.
Title:	Oh, How Can I Keep from Singing?
Voicing:	SATB
Accomp:	a cappella
Text:	Traditional folk hymn - My life flows on in endless song above life's lamentation.
Range:	d4-f5, Bb3-c5, db3-f4, gb2-db4
Difficulty:	MED

Style: An expressive setting of this folk hymn text. The harmonies are traditional but punctuated with sharp dissonances resulting from suspensions, added tones, and passing tones. In a moderate tempo, the shifting meter is used to treat the text underlay carefully. The texture is primarily contrapuntal. Through-composed but sectional, each verse receiving individual treatment.

Comments: Highly recommended. A very expressive setting. The voice parts lie well within the ranges of high school voices. This would work well with either a large chorus or a small ensemble.

Publisher:	Oxford University Press 94.335
Usage:	Secular concert
Date:	1988
Level:	H.S.

81

Composer:	Haufrecht, Herbert
Title:	Dispute Among Divines - #4 from BENJAMIN FRANKLIN
Voicing:	SATB
Accomp:	a cappella
Text:	Secular
Range:	c#4-g5, a3-d5, f3-f4, a2-d4
Difficulty:	MED

Style: This piece moves from a slow, legato opening section to a faster, more marcato ending. 3/4 meter is employed throughout. The texture is primarily contrapuntal. Interesting use of non-traditional harmonies.

Comments: A well written piece featuring interesting text painting.

Publisher:	Rongwen Music, Inc. R.M. 3534
Duration:	1:10
Usage:	Secular concert
Date:	1974
Level:	H.S.

82

Composer:	Healey, Derek
Title:	There is one Body
Voicing:	SATB
Accomp:	Organ and Electronic tape
Text:	Sacred - Ephesians 4:4 There is one body and one spirit.
Range:	d4-Bb4, d4-Bb4
Difficulty:	MED

Style:	Avant garde. Tone clusters, improvisation, and sharp dissonances. Most singing consists of ad lib repetitions of a short 2-pitch motive. Organ part is complex.
Comments:	Not difficult for singers. An effective, work but requires a good accompanist.

Publisher:	Chanteclair Music (Gordon V. Thompson Ltd.)
Usage:	Secular - sacred concert
Date:	1975
Level:	H.S. - college

83

Composer:	Healey, Derek
Title:	O King Enthroned on High *
Voicing:	SATB
Accomp:	Organ
Text:	Sacred
Range:	d4-c#5, b3-c#5, d3-c#4, g2-c#4
Difficulty:	Easy

Style:	The first section of the piece is sung in unison by all voices. Following a brief interlude, the chorus returns singing a brief closing section in chordal style. Fairly traditional harmonies; mildly dissonant.
Comments:	The piece is simple, short and cohesive. Best suited for church use.

Publisher: Augsburg Pub House
Usage: Sacred concert
Date: 1976
Level: H.S.

84

Composer: Hemberg, Eskil
Title: Signposts
Voicing: SATB
Accomp: a cappella
Text: Sacred - Psalms 60:2 and 73
Range: g#4-a(b)5, f#3-e(a)5, db3-a(b)4, f#2-c4 extreme ranges in all voices
Difficulty: Med Diff

Style: A set of three pieces in avant garde style. Meter and rhythmic values are indicated. Pitch is sometimes indicated; at other times only approximate ranges are suggested. Glissandi are used. 1st and 3rd pieces utilize canonic techniques. Some use of speech and modified sprechstimme.

Comments: A well written set. Avant garde but accessible to the h.s. chorus.

Publisher: Walton Music Corp 11842
Usage: Sacred - secular concert
Date: 1969
Level: H.S.

85

Composer: Hindemith, Paul
Title: Since all is Passing   #3 of SIX CHANSONS
Voicing: SATB
Accomp: a cappella
Text: Secular - French (English) Since all is passing, retain the melodies that wander by us.
Range: e4-e5, b3-b4, f#3-f4, a2-c4
Difficulty: Med Easy

Style: Homophonic. Short and lively in 6/8 meter. Internal phrasing and dynamic coloration are a vital part of this piece. Melodic line is in soprano; other voice parts have conjunct movement and are quite singable.

Comments:	This is a short classic accessible to most h.s. choirs. Requires careful tuning, excellent diction and attention to phrasing.
Publisher:	Schott & Co 10456
Usage:	Secular concert
Date:	1939
Level:	H.S. - college

86

Composer:	Hopson, Hal H.
Title:	A Prayer of Supplication
Voicing:	SATB
Accomp:	a cappella
Text:	Sacred - Janet McGinnis Noble
Range:	d4-e5, b3-b4, d#3-e4, g2-b3
Difficulty:	MED

Style:	The anthem opens with a somewhat astringent harmonic treatment in open fourths and fifths, then proceeds to a short imitative section. A Brief middle section relieves the harmonic tension with a much less dissonant treatment of a short "Kyrie eleison" statement. The rhythmic movement of the piece is slow, in quarter- and eighth-note movement with frequent use of quarter-note triplet figures.
Comments:	A particularly effective setting of an interesting text. Good concert material--would be useful for a very strong church youth choir.
Publisher:	G.I.A. Publications, Inc. G-1977
Usage:	Sacred - secular concert
Date:	1975
Level:	H.S.

87

Composer:	Hopson, Hal H.
Title:	Come, Make a Joyful Sound
Voicing:	SATB
Accomp:	Piano or organ
Text:	Sacred - Psalm 100 and Isaiah 64:8
Range:	c4-f5, Bb3-c5, c3-eb4, c3-d4
Difficulty:	Med Easy

Style: The harmony is mildly dissonant with frequent added tones. Opening with unison voices, the piece moves through a short duet between men's and women's voices before the introduction of a central chorale-like B section. After a brief da capo, the work concludes with a forte "alleluia" exclamation.

Comments: An effective work for a church youth choir. Well written for young voices.

Publisher: Sacred Music Press S-287
Usage: Church service or concert
Date: 1982
Level: H.S.

88

Composer: Hurd, David
Title: Six Alleluia Canons
Voicing: S(ATB)
Accomp: a cappella-optional piano or organ, handbells
Text: Alleluia
Range: Bb3-f5
Difficulty: Med Easy

Style: These are four-voice canons that may be sung a cappella or with keyboard accompaniment. The melodic line is quite singable; the resulting harmonies are sometimes punctuated by sharp dissonances but move to consonant cadences. Nos. 3 and 4 are in 6/8 and 6/4, respectively, and are more rhythmically challenging than the other four.

Comments: Useful for girls' chorus or mixed choir. These would make interesting music for a processional or to begin a Christmas concert.

Publisher: G.I.A. Publications, Inc. - G3149
Usage: Christmas or general sacred
Date: 1988
Level: H.S.

89

Composer: Hutcheson, Jere
Title: Lament for a Lost Child
Voicing: SATB
Accomp: a cappella

Text:	Secular - nonsense sounds: vowels, consonants, etc. No text.
Range:	f#4-g5(Bb5), a3-f5, f#3-d4, e2-e4
Difficulty:	MED

Style: Avant garde: glissandi, tone clusters, and other special effects are called for. Lots of sharp dissonances. Notes are approached by step and are not difficult to find. No real melodic line except for short phrase by soprano soloist.

Comments: Requires a pretty wide range in all voices. H.S. choirs can handle this. Success depends on the manner in which it is presented to the group. Good teaching tool for avant garde music.

Publisher:	Walton Music 2921
Duration:	4:
Usage:	Secular concert
Date:	1974
Level:	H.S. - college

90

Composer:	Ives, Charles
Title:	Easter Carol *
Voicing:	SATB
Accomp:	Organ
Text:	Sacred
Range:	db4-a5, b3-d5, db4-g4, f#2-e4
Difficulty:	MED

Style: Homophonic. Traditional, sentimental church style from late 19th century. ABA form; soli section for quartet is center of piece.

Comments: A good introduction to Ives for h.s. singers. Traditional harmony with Ivesian idiosyncracies thrown in. Accessible to average or better h.s. choirs.

Publisher:	Associated Music Publishers, Inc. A-684
Usage:	Sacred - secular concert
Date:	1973
Level:	H.S. - college

91

Composer:	Jackson, Hanley

Title: Vignettes of the Plains *
Voicing: SATB
Accomp: Electronic tape
Text: Secular - Four short Indian poems
Range: c4-f5, g3-d5, Bb2-g4, f2-a3
Difficulty: Med Dif

Style: Avant garde in that the electronic tape is used. Voice treatment is dissonant but fairly traditional. Tone clusters are used in first vignette only. Work consists of four short settings of Indian poems. I and IV are scored for SATB; II for SST; and III for TTB.

Comments: An interesting and accessible work. Jackson's work utilizes a good bit of unison, and the part writing is quite singable.

Publisher: Shawnee Press Inc A 1438
Duration: 6:40
Usage: Secular concert
Date: 1978
Level: H.S. - college

92

Composer: Jackson, Hanley
Title: Psalm XXI
Voicing: SATB
Accomp: a cappella
Text: Sacred
Range: d4-eb5, a3-c5, g2-c4
Difficulty: Med Dif

Style: Avant garde. Involves audience as well as the choir. Various contemporary techniques are used including chord clusters, whispers, and the use of various vocal syllables. The hymn "Herzliebster Jesu" is sung at various times by the choir and the audience The narration is an integral part of the work.

Comments: An effective and not overly difficult avant garde work. Well written; deserves performance.

Publisher: Walton Music Corp
Usage: Sacred - secular concert
Date: 1977
Level: H.S.

93

Composer:	Jackson, Hanley
Title:	A Child's Ghetto
Voicing:	SATB
Accomp:	Electronic tape
Text:	Secular - Snow descends, why must it go so soon...
Range:	e4-d5, c4-b4, c3-e4, c3-b3
Difficulty:	MED

Style: Avant garde; combines electronic tape with chorus utilizing both conventional singing and unusual sound effects (hissing, tongue clicks, tone clusters, etc.). Opens with pointillistic writing between voices; middle section is somewhat traditional in style. Ends on a unison as tape fades out.

Comments: Highly effective work in this medium; accessible to the average or better h.s. choir. Careful introduction and explanation is important for both choir and audience.

Publisher:	Walton Music Corp 2916
Duration:	6:
Usage:	Secular concert
Date:	1972
Level:	H.S. - college

94

Composer:	Jennings, Kenneth
Title:	With a Voice of Singing
Voicing:	SATB
Accomp:	a cappella
Text:	Sacred - Isaiah 48:20b; Psalm 66:1-2
Range:	f4-a5, b3-d5, e3-f#4, a2-c#4
Difficulty:	MED

Style: This piece is lively and rhythmic with frequent meter changes. Homophonic throughout. A contrasting middle section is in a slow, chant-like style and is set for men's voices. A festive and exciting work.

Comments: Requires clean articulation. Accessible to average or better h.s choir. Excellent program material. Harmonies are generally quite traditional.

Publisher:	Augsburg Publishing House 11-1379
Usage:	Sacred - secular concert

Date: 1964
Level: H.S. - college

95

Composer: Jennings, Kenneth
Title: Arise, Shine, for Thy Light has Come
Voicing: SATB
Accomp: a cappella
Text: Sacred - Isaiah 60:1-3
Range: e4-f(g)5, e4-c5, e3-e4, b2-c#4
Difficulty: MED

Style: Homophonic throughout with frequently changing meters. In ABA form; the central section is set for men alone. A rhythmic and festive work. 2nds and 7ths are used extensively.

Comments: Good material for an opener.   Accessible to the average or better h.s. choir.

Publisher: Augsburg Publishing House 11-1498
Usage: Sacred - secular concert
Date: 1967
Level: H.S.

96

Composer: Jennings, Kenneth
Title: American Indian Songs
Voicing: SATB
Accomp: Piano
Text: Secular - seven Indian poems
Range: Bb3-a5, a2-c5, Bb2-a4, g2-c4
Difficulty: MED

Style: Most of these settings are short mood pieces. Open 5ths and 4ths are quite common. The piano accompaniment is an integral part of the compositions and helps to set the mood for each new text. Choral writing is basically conjunct and quite singable.

Comments: An interesting and unusual group. Good material for variety on the choral concert. Accessible to most h.s. choirs.

Publisher: Walton Music Corp. 2992

SATB

Usage:	Secular concert
Date:	1976
Level:	H.S.

97

Composer:	Jergenson, Dale
Title:	The Lament of Job
Voicing:	SATB
Accomp:	a cappella
Text:	Sacred - Job - Oh, who will bring back to me the months that have gone, and the days when God was my guardian
Range:	e4-e5, b3-b4, d3-g4, g2-d4
Difficulty:	Med Dif

Style: Avant garde. Combines tone clusters, speech chorus, improvisation, non-traditional vocal sounds, and traditional choral singing. Most of the work utilizes indeterminate pitches, but the opening and closing sections are in strict 4-pt notation.

Comments: An intriguing work. The piece was written for a h.s. madrigal group. An effective piece that will help students to better understand avant garde music.

Publisher:	G. Schirmer
Usage:	Secular-sacred concert
Date:	1975
Level:	H.S.

98

Composer:	Johanson, Sven-Eric
Title:	Fancies I
Voicing:	SATB
Accomp:	Piano
Text:	Secular texts by Shakespeare
Range:	d4-g5, a3-c5, d3-g4, g2-d4
Difficulty:	Med Dif

Style: Utilizes a mixture of contrapuntal and homophonic textures. Harmonies are fairly contemporary but only mildly dissonant. Lively rhythms with some use of mixed meters, but rhythmically pieces are not problematic. This is the first of a set of two Fancies by Johanson.

Comments: These pieces require careful preparation and sensitive interpretation. Excellent material for the chamber choir.

Publisher: AB Carl Gehrmans Musikforlag (Walton Music Corp)
Usage: Secular concert
Date: 1974
Level: H.S. - college

99

Composer: Johanson, Sven-Eric
Title: Fancies II
Voicing: SATB
Accomp: Piano
Text: Secular texts by Shakespeare
Range: d4-g5, g#3-c5, e3-e4, a2-d4
Difficulty: Med Dif

Style: This is the second of a set of two Fancies by Johanson. Set I includes: 1) Sylvia, 2) Under the Greenwood Tree, 3) Blow Thou Winter Wind, 4) Fancy, 5) O Mistress Mine. Set II includes: 6) Lovers Love the Spring, 7) Winter, 8) Dirge, 9) Hark! Hark! the lark.

Comments: Good material for a madrigal group or chamber choir.

Publisher: AB Carl Gehrman Musikforlag (Walton Music Corp)
Usage: Secular concert
Date: 1974
Level: H.S. - college

100

Composer: Kreutz, Robert E.
Title: How Glorious Your Name, O Lord
Voicing: SATB
Accomp: a cappella
Text: Sacred - Psalm 8 - How glorious is your name throughout all the earth
Range: d4-g5(Bb5), a3-eb5, f3-g4, g2-d4   High tone in sop. occurs only once.
Difficulty: Med Dif

Style: Driving rhythms with frequently changing meter. Sectional piece which includes a short recapitulation. Primarily homophonic with short contrapuntal sections. Mildly dissonant. Melodic movement is conjunct for the most part.

Comments: Would be a good contest selection. Appealing to young choirs because of the rhythmic fervor.

Publisher: World Library Pub. Inc. 7602-8
Usage: Sacred-secular concert
Date: 1979
Level: H.S.

101

Composer: Kreutz, Robert E.
Title: The Night Will Never Stay
Voicing: SATB
Accomp: Piano
Text: Secular - The night will never stay, the night will still go by
Range: c4-g5, ab3-Bb4, c3-f4, g2-Bb3
Difficulty: Easy

Style: A slow, quiet, mystical piece; very descriptive of text. Interesting ostinato figure in piano accompaniment. Tonal; dissonances occur from added tones and passing tones. Parts are quite singable and lie well within the range of h.s. singers.

Comments: Good, accessible piece for any h.s. choir. A lovely setting in 20th-century harmonic language. Somewhat neo-romantic.

Publisher: Shawnee Press A 1479
Usage: Secular concert
Date: 1978
Level: H.S.

102

Composer: Lamb, Gordon H.
Title: Aleatory Psalm *
Voicing: SATB
Accomp: a cappella
Text: Sacred - Psalm 150
Range: c4-f#5, c4-a4,
Difficulty: Med Dif

Style: Avant garde; utilizes chord clusters, approximate pitches, speaking parts, glissandi, repeated motives, and prescribed pitches. Alternates between strictly measured sections and those that are freely interpreted. At times the speaking parts are mingled with singing in a contrapuntal style.

Comments: An interesting utilization of a number of avant garde techniques.

Publisher: World Library Pub. CA-4003-8
Usage: Sacred-secular concert
Date: 1973
Level: H.S.

103

Composer: Larsen, Libby
Title: She's Like a Swallow
Voicing: SATB
Accomp: Piano, flute
Text: Secular - traditional
Range: d3-eb5, ab3-c5, c3-g4, g2-eb4
Difficulty: MED

Style: The melody is set in the style of a Scottish folksong and is introduced by a tenor solo; extensive use of paired duets either in alternation or in opposition to the other voices. Except for the improvisatory introduction, the meter is 6/8 throughout. There are no rhythmic problems. The introduction calls for either flute or soprano solo; the piano accompaniment requires a strong pianist, but nicely complements the vocal writing. The harmonies are tonal; extensive use of seventh chords.

Comments: There is some divisi writing in the alto and bass parts. The solo flute and piano accompaniment make this a particularly appealing work.

Publisher: E.C. Schirmer 3107
Duration: 3:25
Usage: Secular concert
Date: 1988
Level: H.S.

104

Composer: Larsson, Lars-Erik
Title: Birds are Never Soaring Too High
Voicing: SATB
Accomp: a cappella

SATB

Text:	Secular
Range:	db4-Bb5, a3-eb4, d3-ab4, a2-c4
Difficulty:	Med Dif

Style: A lively and rhythmic setting characterized by eighth- and sixteenth-note repetitive figures. Basically contrapuntal. Traditional harmonies with some mild dissonances.

Comments: An attractive work characterized by driving rhythms. Interesting program material.

Publisher:	Walton Music Corp.
Usage:	Secular concert
Date:	1969
Level:	H.S.

105

Composer:	Lekberg, Sven
Title:	Four Carols for a Holy Night
Voicing:	SATB
Accomp:	a cappella
Text:	Sacred - 1) Sing Noel; 2) Earth So Lovely; 3) The Little Jesus Boy; 4) These are the Blossoms
Range:	c#4-g#5, a3-c4, db3-f#4, gb2-d4
Difficulty:	MED

Style: Homophonic. The first piece is in a lively, jubilant 6/8. The second piece is a reverent, more subdued work in 4/4. The third piece is set in a gently flowing 3/4, and the final piece has alternating meters and tempi. Fairly traditional harmonies with some altered chords.

Comments: A well written Christmas set. Good program material.

Publisher:	G. Schirmer, Inc. 11646
Usage:	Sacred secular concert - Christmas
Date:	1969
Level:	H.S.

106

Composer:	Lovelock, William
Title:	Who Is at My Window?
Voicing:	SATB

Accomp: organ
Text: Sacred - Who is at my window? Go! Who calls there like a stranger?
                 Lord, I am here, a wretched mortal.
Range: c4-a5, b3-c#5, d3-f#4, f#2-c4
Difficulty: Med Easy

Style: Through-composed with a short repeat of opening statement before a
                 concluding coda. Primarily homophonic texture. Tonal, very mild
                 dissonances. Eighth- and quarter-note movement with quarter=60. A
                 quiet, reflective work.

Comments: A beautiful setting of a unique text. Nice phrasing; sustained lines.

Publisher: Walton Music Corp
Usage: Sacred-secular concert
Date: 1978
Level: H.S.

107

Composer: Manz, Paul O.
Title: E'en So, Lord Jesus, Quickly Come
Voicing: SATB
Accomp: a cappella
Text: Sacred - Revelation 22
Range: eb4-f5(Bb5), ab3-db5, f3-f4(ab4), ab2(db2)-eb4
Difficulty: MED

Style: Frequently changing meters; opens in an adagio and accelerates in the
                 middle section. Homophonic. Flowing, legato phrases. Rich, moderately
                 dissonant chords are employed.

Comments: A beautiful, legato work which would display the expressive abilities of
                 the chorus.

Publisher: Concordia Publishing House
Usage: Sacred - secular concert
Date: 1954
Level: H.S.

108

Composer: Mathias, William
Title: It Was a Lover and his Lass

Voicing:	SATB
Accomp:	Piano
Text:	Secular - Shakespeare - <u>As You Like It</u>
Range:	c4-e5, c4-e5
Difficulty:	MED

Style: This is a clever setting of the familiar Shakespeare text. The men whistle throughout; they first introduce a motive that is repeated between the first three verses, then accompany the women's voices in verse 4. The sopranos sing the first verse in unison; the altos sing the second verse, and the third and fourth verses are sung in canon with the aforementioned whistling undergirding the fourth verse. The accompaniment is in a continuous rhythmic pattern throughout.

Comments: A novel and fun piece. This could be done with a girls' chorus utilizing recorders on the whistling part. It does require adept whistlers.

Publisher:	Oxford University Pres 52.028
Usage:	Secular concert
Date:	1980
Level:	H.S. - College

109

Composer:	Maw, Nicholas
Title:	Jig from FIVE IRISH SONGS
Voicing:	SATB
Accomp:	a cappella
Text:	Secular folk-song - That winter love spoke and we raised no objection, at Easter twas daisies all light and affectionate
Range:	c4-a5, a3-f#5, c3-ab4, a2-d4
Difficulty:	Med Dif

Style: Continuously moving melodic line in a rapid 6/8 constantly shifts between the 4 voices. Contrapuntal. Diatonic lines characterized by staccato eighth-note movement.

Comments: Delightful folksong setting. A little long and somewhat demanding. Accessible to mature h.s. group.

Publisher:	Boosey & Hawkes 5911
Usage:	Secular concert
Date:	1973
Level:	H.S. - college

110

Composer:	Maw, Nicholas
Title:	Popular Song #3 of FIVE IRISH SONGS *
Voicing:	SATB
Accomp:	a cappella
Text:	Secular folksong - The cuckoo is pretty, sings as it flies...
Range:	d4-g5, a3-e5, c#3-f4, g2-a3
Difficulty:	MED

Style: Mixture of homophonic and contrapuntal textures; folk melody is set against constantly changing choral accompaniment. Lively, 6/8 movement. Mildly dissonant. A spirited, playful piece.

Comments: Accessible to the average h.s. chorus. An interesting, fun arrangement of an Irish folksong.

Publisher:	Boosey & Hawkes
Usage:	Secular concert
Date:	1974
Level:	H.S. - college

111

Composer:	McCray, James
Title:	Passages
Voicing:	SATB
Accomp:	Piano - chimes
Text:	Secular - Walt Whitman
Range:	c4-e5, c4-d5, c3-e4, c3-e4
Difficulty:	Med Easy

Style: The octavo is sectional and episodic with short piano interludes between successive vocal statements. Tonal with mild dissonances achieved through passing tones and added tones. Frequent use of parallel chords. Effective text painting is created through tempo changes, changes in melodic direction and the accompaniment. Throughout the piece, recitative-like statements contrast with more moving and developmental choral sections.

Comments: A sensitive setting of this Whitman text. Well written for high school voices. Both the text and the music require a mature and thoughtful performance by the choir. The voicing is really for SAB choir with very limited divisi in the bass part.

SATB

Publisher:	National Music Publishers NMP-177
Usage:	Secular concert
Date:	1986
Level:	H.S.

112

Composer:	McCray, James
Title:	A Child Said
Voicing:	SATB
Accomp:	Piano - oboe
Text:	Secular - Walt Whitman
Range:	d4-g5, Bb3-e5, d3-f4, Bb2-d4
Difficulty:	MED

Style: This piece opens with an oboe solo, followed by a unison setting of the first verse of text. Through-composed with a slightly different setting for each verse of text. Mildly dissonant with conjunct melodic lines. There is extensive use of cluster tones in the syncopated accompaniment. The tempo is quite slow, and the piece calls for expressive singing.

Comments: The work requires good breath control and careful attention to phrasing.

Publisher:	National Music Publishers NMP-151
Usage:	Secular concert
Date:	1984
Level:	H.S.

113

Composer:	McCray, James
Title:	Jubilate Deo
Voicing:	SATB
Accomp:	Handbells
Text:	Sacred - Psalm 100 - O be joyful in the Lord all ye lands
Range:	e4-e5, ab3-e5, e3-e4, ab2-e4
Difficulty:	Med Easy

Style: Homophonic. Mildly dissonant, primarily through added tones. Moves at a moderate tempo with alternating meters. In ABA form; the outer sections are in a fanfare style; mid-section is slower and features soli and SSA singing. Conclusion of the middle section is built on a moving tone cluster.

Comments: An interesting work for h.s. chorus. Will sound well and is accessible to most h.s. groups.

Publisher: Tetra Music Corp AB 953 (Alexander Broude)
Usage: Sacred-secular concert
Date: 1981
Level: H.S.

114

Composer: McCray, James
Title: I Will Give Thanks to the Lord
Voicing: SATB
Accomp: Handbell choir
Text: Sacred
Range: c4-e5, a3-e5, c3-e4, c3-e4
Difficulty: Easy

Style: A rather short anthem utilizing unison singing and random (prescribed pitches) improvisatory handbell ringing. Very short homophonic section. Favored dissonance in both voices and bells is the major 2nd.

Comments: Not a classic, but utilizes interesting timbres through the use of the handbells. Would make interesting program material.

Publisher: Tetra Music Corp AB888 (Alexander Broude)
Usage: Sacred-secular concert
Date: 1980
Level: H.S.

115

Composer: McKay, David P.
Title: Come Sing Madrigals *
Voicing: SATB
Accomp: Trumpets and Trombones
Text: Secular - Come sing madrigals, oh come away, let's sport afield
Range: e4-a5, Bb3-d5, g3-g4, gb2-c4 Soprano and tenor lie a little high
Difficulty: Med Dif

SATB

Style:	Highly rhythmic with a lively tempo. Homophonic throughout. Some use of bitonality and added tones. Middle section is slower and more lyrical.
Comments:	For the fine h.s. choir this would be excellent program material. The brass provides a pleasant divergence in timbre. Because of the brass, a fairly large choir is required.
Publisher:	Shawnee Press Inc.
Duration:	4:15
Usage:	Secular concert
Date:	1974
Level:	H.S. - college

116

Composer:	Mechem, Kirke
Title:	The Lighthearted Lovers
Voicing:	SATB
Accomp:	Piano
Text:	Secular - John Dryden - Fair Iris I love and hourly I die, but not for a lisp, nor a languishing eye; She's fickle and false, and thus we agree...
Range:	e4-a5, b3-e5, e3-a4, a2-e4
Difficulty:	Diff
Style:	Mildly dissonant with frequent added tones. Rhythmic and in a brisk tempo throughout. Extensive use of paired duets between men's and women's voices. A mixture of contrapuntal and homophonic textures.
Comments:	An exciting but demanding work. The piece is best suited for use with large festival choirs in the high school setting.
Publisher:	G. Schirmer 12477
Usage:	High school festival
Date:	1983
Level:	H.S. - college

117

Composer:	Mechem, Kirke
Title:	Laughing Song
Voicing:	SATB
Accomp:	a cappella
Text:	Secular poem by William Blake - When the green woods laugh with the voice of joy.

Range:	c4-a5, Bb3-e5, c3-a4, g2-e4 Tenor lies quite high.
Difficulty:	Diff

Style: Through-composed. Imitative, contrapuntal writing interspersed with short homophonic sections. Linear part-writing is quite singable. Sharp dissonances result from the combination of the parts. Frequently shifting meters. Playful spirit in keeping with the text.

Comments: Accessible to a strong h.s. choir with good tenor section. If each part is treated as a solo line, much of the difficulty of the harmonic structure can be overcome.

Publisher:	Mercury Music Corp MC554
Usage:	Secular concert
Date:	1968
Level:	H.S. - college

118

Composer:	Medema, Ken
Title:	Moses
Voicing:	SATB
Accomp:	Piano
Text:	Sacred - A free paraphrase of Moses' dialogue in the wilderness.
Range:	d4-g5, c4-f5, d3-g4, a2-f4
Difficulty:	MED

Style: An extended narrative including some speech singing. Rhythmic. Alternation between unison and homophonic sections Basically in a semi-rock-jazz style. Closes with a schmaltzy ending.

Comments: Primarily useful for a church youth choir. The imaginative and highly rhythmic treatment makes this a really fun piece for h.s. age choirs.

Publisher:	Word Music Inc.
Usage:	Sacred - church youth choir
Date:	1974
Level:	H.S.

119

Composer:	Mennin, Peter
Title:	Crossing the Han River
Voicing:	SATB

Accomp:	a cappella
Text:	Secular poem by Kiana Kang-Hu - Away from home I was longing for news...
Range:	d4-g5, a3-b4, d3-g4, a2-d#4
Difficulty:	Med Dif

Style: Contrapuntal. Flowing movement throughout. Begins quietly and crescendos to climax, followed by a short, quiet ending. Effective use of parallel octaves between alto and soprano in mid-section.

Comments: Very descriptive setting of the text. Long phrases require good breath control. An exciting work.

Publisher:	Carl Fischer Inc.
Usage:	Secular concert
Date:	1948
Level:	H.S. - college

120

Composer:	Moe, Daniel
Title:	Psalm Concertato Pt.II *
Voicing:	SATB
Accomp:	Brass and string bass
Text:	Sacred. Psalm 103:1,2 - Bless the Lord, O My Soul
Range:	eb4-f5, a3-eb5, c3-f4, f2-d4
Difficulty:	MED

Style: Short legato phrases. Opens at mp and slowly crescendos to ff. Homophonic . Major 2nds and 7ths are prevalent. Contrasts with the louder and more rhythmic outer sections of the full work.

Comments: Accessible piece for h.s. choir. Chorale style is good for developing a sense of phrasing.

Publisher:	Augsburg Publishing House 11-633
Usage:	Secular-sacred concert
Date:	1970
Level:	H.S. - college

121

Composer:	Moe, Daniel
Title:	Hosanna to the Son of David

Voicing:	SATB
Accomp:	Organ
Text:	Sacred - Matthew 21:9
Range:	d4-g5, a3-e5, d3-g#4, g2-d4
Difficulty:	MED

Style: ABA form. Outer sections are homophonic; some contrapuntal writing in mid-section. Short exclamatory phrases. Added tones result in some sharp dissonances. Rhythmic and driving.

Comments: A fine piece for the mature h.s. choir.

Publisher:	Mercury Music Corp
Usage:	Sacred - secular concert: Palm Sunday or advent
Date:	1956
Level:	H.S. - college

122

Composer:	Moe, Daniel
Title:	Psalm Concertato Pt.I *
Voicing:	SATB
Accomp:	Brass and String bass
Text:	Sacred. Psalm 150: 1,2,6 - Let everything that has breath, praise ye the Lord.
Range:	f4-g5, d4-Eb5, e3-f#4, Eb3-e4
Difficulty:	MED

Style: Highly rhythmic. Short, exclamatory phrases. Tension builds and is resolved in final two phrases of work. Some disjunct melodic writing. Major 2nds and 7ths are prevalent, as are quarter-note triplets.

Comments: May be performed alone or as a part of the entire work. An exciting piece but requires good brass players and a strong choir.

Publisher:	Augsburg Publishing House 11-632
Usage:	Secular-sacred concert
Date:	1970
Level:	H.S. - college

123

Composer:	Moe, Daniel
Title:	Psalm Concertato Pt.III *

Voicing:	SATB
Accomp:	Brass and String bass
Text:	Sacred-Psalm 47:1,7 - Clap your hands, all ye people
Range:	d4-Ab5, c4-Eb5, d3- f4, c3-d4
Difficulty:	Med Dif

Style:	Highly rhythmic with alternation between duple and triple meter. Frequent simultaneous pairing of bass-alto and soprano-tenor voices in an interesting contrapuntal texture. ABA form. Mid-section is somewhat more lyrical than the exclamatory outer sections.

Comments:	The most difficult of the three movements. Requires a mature and aggressive choir.

Publisher:	Augsburg Publishing House 11-634
Usage:	Secular-sacred concert
Date:	1970
Level:	H.S. - college

124

Composer:	Moe, Daniel
Title:	Stranger, Share Our Fire *
Voicing:	SATB
Accomp:	a cappella
Text:	Sacred poem by James Hearst - Stranger, share our fire, here's a sop of stew . . .
Range:	d4-g5, c4-c5, d3-f4, f2-d4
Difficulty:	Easy

Style:	Opens homophonically, then moves through a short unison section to a two-part contrapuntal section. Second half of piece is homophonic with baritone solo. Mild dissonances, added tones. Frequently shifting meter. Tempo is moderate.

Comments:	Anthem based on a contemporary hymn. Work would sound well with a young choir.

Publisher:	Augsburg Publishing House 11-0529
Usage:	Sacred-secular concert
Date:	1969
Level:	H.S.

125

Composer:	Moe, Daniel
Title:	Let Your Eye be to the Lord
Voicing:	SATB
Accomp:	a cappella
Text:	Sacred poem by William Penn
Range:	c4-g5, Bb3-c5, c3-f4, f2-d4
Difficulty:	Med Dif

Style:

Through-composed. Opens with solo statement of melody built on a pentatonic scale. A two-part canon follows and closes in 4-pt harmony. Added tones and use of canon result in frequent major 2nds and other dissonances, but these are generally mild.

Comments:

Introduces students to dissonance while maintaining a solid, tonal framework.

Publisher:	Augsburg Pub House 11-0544
Usage:	Sacred - secular concert
Date:	1973
Level:	H.S. - college

126

Composer:	Mollicone, Henry
Title:	Lullaby from A CHRISTMAS CELEBRATION
Voicing:	SATB
Accomp:	Organ and flute
Text:	Sacred
Range:	d3-g5, b3-b4, d3-e4, g#2-b3
Difficulty:	MED

Style:

Set in 6/8 meter, the repetitive rocking rhythm in both the vocal parts and accompaniment captures the spirit of a lullaby. The solo flute introduces the melody, which is then sung in its entirety by a solo soprano. The texture is a mixture of contrapuntal and homophonic styles. The "lulay" repetitions are set in a question-answer pattern that changes with each new verse. Through-composed; tonal, but mildly dissonant.

Comments:

Good Christmas material for either school or church. Easily accessible. The flute solo nicely complements both the accompaniment and vocal parts.

Publisher:	E.C. Schirmer 4242
Usage:	Christmas Concert or Anthem
Date:	1987
Level:	H.S. - Adult

127

Composer:	Mollicone, Henry
Title:	Send Forth, O God, Thy Light and Truth
Voicing:	SATB
Accomp:	a cappella
Text:	Sacred - John Quincy Adams
Range:	eb4-f5, c4-c5, e3-e4, a2-b3
Difficulty:	MED

Style: Homophonic. Sustained and flowing in a slow tempo. Tonal harmonies with frequent suspension figures adding mild dissonance. The two verses of text are in strophic form concluding with an extended coda.

Comments: All of the voice parts lie comfortably within the range of high school singers. A beautiful and effective anthem for church and concert use.

Publisher:	E.C. Schirmer ECS 3083
Usage:	Sacred concert, Epiphany anthem
Date:	1983
Level:	H.S.- College

128

Composer:	Monhardt, Maurice
Title:	Let the People Praise Thee
Voicing:	SATB
Accomp:	a cappella
Text:	Sacred - Psalm 67
Range:	c4-g5, a3-eb5, eb3-g4, g2-eb4
Difficulty:	Med Dif

Style: A rhythmic, fanfare anthem. In ABA form, the outer sections move rapidly, while the central section is in a slower chorale style. Somewhat dissonant with vacillation between the major and minor modes. A short ostinato figure creates rhythmic tension between the bass line and the upper three voices.

Comments: An exciting piece for a good, well balanced mixed chorus.

Publisher: Augsburg Publishing House 10-0610
Usage: Sacred-secular concert
Date: 1963
Level: H.S. - college

129

Composer: Nagel, Robert
Title: Triptych *
Voicing: SATB
Accomp: Piano &/or Organ &/or Brass quartet
Text: Sacred: Psalm 117 & Revelation 7:12. 1) Glory to God, 2) O Praise the
               Lord, 3) Glory and Blessing
Range: e4-g5, Bb3-d5, f3-g4, f1-c4
Difficulty: MED

Style: Primarily homophonic throughout. Added tones give a little edge to the
               traditional harmony. Three short movements with brass accompaniment.
               Rhythmic movement is mostly in half and quarter notes. Fanfare quality
               in each movement.

Comments: Would add variety to programming. Brass parts are not difficult.

Publisher: Edward B. Marks
Duration: 4:
Usage: Sacred secular concert
Date: 1972
Level: H.S.

130

Composer: Nelson, Ron
Title: Choral Fanfare for Christmas
Voicing: TTBB or SATB (some divisi)
Accomp: 3 trumpets, 3 trombones and tuba
Text: Sacred
Range: d4-f5, Bb3-c5, f3-e4, Bb2-c4
Difficulty: MED

Style: A fanfare work characterized by driving rhythms. Meter alternates
               between 3/4 and 4/4. Extensive use of major chords. Both homophonic
               and contrapuntal textures are utilized.

SATB

Comments: A good, short piece effective as an opener on a Christmas concert. Provides a variety of timbre for the typical concert.

Publisher: Boosey & Hawkes, Inc.
Usage: Sacred - secular concert - Christmas
Date: 1960
Level: H.S.

131

Composer: Nelson, Ron
Title: Thy Truth is Great
Voicing: SATB
Accomp: Piano or organ
Text: Sacred - Thy truth is great, O Lord, even as the sea
Range: ab3-g5(Bb5), ab3-b4, f3-g4, f2-eb4   Fairly extreme range in soprano line
Difficulty: Med Dif

Style: Frequently changing meters and tempi. Homophonic and contrapuntal textures are utilized. Much use of tertian harmony. Added tones create mild dissonances.

Comments: An interesting, but difficult work. There are a number of rhythmic problems in the piece. Would be a rewarding work for a strong h.s. choir.

Publisher: Boosey & Hawkes, Inc.
Duration: 4:
Usage: Sacred - secular concert
Date: 1973
Level: H.S. - college

132

Composer: Nickson, John A.
Title: Take, Oh Take Those Lips Away
Voicing: SATB
Accomp: a cappella
Text: Secular text by J. Fletcher
Range: f4-g5, c4-c5, eb3-e4, (e)ab2-c#4
Difficulty: Med Easy

Style: A quiet, tender setting of this familiar text. The choral writing is basically homophonic featuring tertian chords with added tones; mildly dissonant. Frequently shifting meter.

Comments: A good piece for showcasing the expressive capabilities of the choral ensemble. Good material for the chamber choir or madrigal group.

Publisher: Plymouth Music Co. PCS -115
Usage: Secular concert
Date: 1978
Level: H.S.

133

Composer: Nystedt, Knut
Title: Listen to Me *
Voicing: SATB
Accomp: a cappella
Text: Sacred - Isaiah 41:13, 17-20; 42:10-12
Range: e4-g5, a3-eb5, b2-g4, Bb2-d4 Tenor tessitura is a little low
Difficulty: Diff

Style: Alternates between homophonic and contrapuntal textures. Tempi are slow to moderate with frequently changing meters. 2nds, 4ths and 7ths are common, creating a contemporary sound, but the piece is only mildly dissonant. The closing section employs extensive use of 16th-note melismas in all voices.

Comments: Only the mature h.s. choir should attempt this work. Requires good readers.

Publisher: Augsburg Publishing House 11-0569
Usage: Sacred - secular concert
Date: 1979
Level: H.S. - college

134

Composer: Parker, Alice
Title: I Saw a Stable - #2 of CAROLS TO PLAY AND SING
Voicing: SATB
Accomp: Organ and Percussion
Text: Sacred poem by Mary E. Coleridge - I saw a stable, low and very bare.
Range: d4-d5, g3-a4, d3-e4, a2-b3

SATB

Difficulty: Med Easy

Style: Homophonic. Quite slow and soft. Major and minor 2nds and quartal
                     harmonies add a mysterious quality to the work. Range of melodic line
                     is restricted throughout.

Comments: Readily accessible to the H.S. choir. Good Christmas program material.

Publisher: E.C. Schirmer 2780
Usage: Christmas
Date: 1971
Level: H.S.

135

Composer: Paul, David
Title: Numbers in a Row
Voicing: SATB
Accomp: a cappella
Text: Secular - The numbers 1-12
Range: c4-g5, g#3-d5, d3-eb4, ab2-c4
Difficulty: Diff

Style: Twelve-tone music approached with tongue-in-cheek humour. Two short
                     pieces, both of which are based on the same row. #1 sounds like a
                     boogie-woogie melody. Finger-snapping, speech, and other avant garde
                     vocal sounds are incorporated.

Comments: For the mature h.s. choir this could be a fun work. Would be good ear
                     training material and would make novel program material.

Publisher: Gordon V. Thompson Ltd.
Usage: Secular concert
Date: 1973
Level: H.S.-college

136

Composer: Peeters, Flor
Title: In Excelsis Gloria!
Voicing: SATB
Accomp: Organ or Piano
Text: Sacred - Christ was born of maiden fair; hark the angels in the air.
Range: d4-d5, Bb3-ab4, e3-d4, a2-g3

Difficulty: Med Easy

Style: Homophonic. Tonal but with a few surprising dissonances. This short, simple setting is in ABA form with the B section set for soprano and tenor alone. An ostinato figure in the bass line creates a rocking effect in the accompaniment.

Comments: This is a quiet anthem with the loudest identified dynamic being mf.

Publisher: Augsburg Publishing House 11-1196
Usage: Sacred concert-Christmas
Date: 1957
Level: H.S.- Jr. High

                                   137

Composer: Persichetti, Vincent
Title: Proverb
Voicing: SATB
Accomp: a cappella
Text: Secular - The rich own the land and the poor own the water
Range: d4-g5, g3-c5, d3-f#4, g2-d4
Difficulty: Med Easy

Style: The piece is set in a slow 3/4 meter. Contrapuntal. Both traditional and non-traditional harmonies are used. Legato and mildly dissonant.

Comments: A sensitive, musical setting of this interesting text from American folklore.

Publisher: Elkan-Vogel Inc. 362-01102
Usage: Secular concert
Date: 1955
Level: H.S.

                                   138

Composer: Persichetti, Vincent
Title: Sing Me the Universal from CELEBRATIONS
Voicing: SATB
Accomp: Wind ensemble or piano
Text: Secular poem by Walt Whitman
Range: c4-e5, a3-a4, e3-e4, g2-d4
Difficulty: MED

Style:	This piece is in 4/4 meter and is set in a moderately fast tempo. Both chordal and contrapuntal styles are included. Contemporary harmonic effects are utilized. The accompaniment provides support, unity, and color to the work.
Comments:	An interesting work with mild dissonances.
Publisher:	Elkan-Vogel, Inc. 362-03228
Usage:	Secular concert
Date:	1967
Level:	H.S.

139

Composer:	Petzold, Johannes
Title:	More Than Raiment *
Voicing:	SATB
Accomp:	a cappella
Text:	Sacred - Matthew 6:25, 26, 28, 29
Range:	d4-f5, a3-d5, d3-f4, a2-c4
Difficulty:	Med Easy

Style:	Homophonic with fairly traditional harmonies; shifting tonal centers. In a moderate tempo; occasional meter changes. Rhythms are relatively simple.
Comments:	A simple, but attractive piece.
Publisher:	Augsburg Publishing House 11-1682
Usage:	Sacred - secular concert
Date:	1973
Level:	H.S.

140

Composer:	Pfautsch, Lloyd
Title:	Who Hath a Right to Sing? from SONGS OF EXPERIENCE
Voicing:	SATB
Accomp:	a cappella with body percussion (handclapping)
Text:	Sacred - Charles Wesley
Range:	eb4-f5, Bb3-eb4, eb3-f4, ab2-eb4
Difficulty:	MED

Style: The work opens with rhythmic handclapping by a small accompaniment group; this percussion continues throughout the piece. The work is rhythmic and utilizes frequently changing meters (alternating between 6/8 and 5/8). Harmonies are diatonic with added tones. Homophonic. Some use of paired duets in dialogue with tutti statements.

Comments: There is some divisi writing in all the voice parts. Good material for a strong, well balanced choir. The body percussion contributes to the interest of the work.

Publisher: Lawson-Gould 52048
Usage: Sacred-secular concert
Date: 1978
Level: H.S. - College

141

Composer: Pfautsch, Lloyd
Title: I Hear America Singing
Voicing: SATB
Accomp: a cappella
Text: Secular - Walt Whitman
Range: c4-a5, c4-d5, d3-g4, g2-d4
Difficulty: MED

Style: The work is rhythmic with changing meters throughout. Frequent use of syncopation and displaced accents. Contrapuntal. Following an opening fanfare, the piece decrescendos into a faster moving A section in which an ostinato figure is established in the bass and tenor lines. The soprano and alto lines carry the principal melodic line and text over this figure. This same treatment returns at the conclusion of the work. Careful attention to text with effective text painting.

Comments: An effective piece. The voice parts lie well within high school ranges. Tonal, but with a generous amount of dissonance through added tones and some quartal harmonies. Highly recommended.

Publisher: Shawnee Press, Inc. A-1092
Duration: 3:00
Usage: Secular concert - Patriotic
Date: 1970
Level: H.S.

142

Composer:	Pfautsch, Lloyd
Title:	Go and Tell John
Voicing:	SATB
Accomp:	a cappella
Text:	Sacred - Matthew 11:4-6
Range:	e4-e5, b3-c#4, e3-e4, a2-b3
Difficulty:	MED

Style: In the style of a Negro spiritual. Rhythmic with some use of syncopation and displaced accents. Primarily contrapuntal with the upper voice set in opposition to the lower voices through most of the work. Sectional, in a modified theme and variations form.

Comments: This is one of Pfautsch's most popular works for high school and church choirs, a lively and exciting piece.

Publisher:	Hope Publishing Co. CY3334
Usage:	Sacred - secular concert
Date:	1970
Level:	H.S.

143

Composer:	Pfautsch, Lloyd
Title:	Come, Thou Fount of Every Blessing
Voicing:	SATB
Accomp:	a cappella
Text:	Sacred - Hymn Text
Range:	d4-f5, a3-e5, d3-f4, g2-d4
Difficulty:	MED

Style: An arrangement of the hymn tune Warrenton (this is not the familiar traditional tune). The setting is a strong, rugged arrangement befitting the tune. The tempo is quite brisk [quarter note = 132]. Contrapuntal. There is judicious use of canonic technique throughout the work. The piece opens in D Major and ends in F Major. Frequent modulation. An exciting and effective setting.

Comments: This piece works well with high school voices and would be suitable for either school or church use.

Publisher:	Lawson-Gould 51074
Usage:	Sacred - secular concert

Date: 1962
Level: H.S.

144

Composer: Pfautsch, Lloyd
Title: Musicks Empire from TRIPTYCH
Voicing: SATB
Accomp: a cappella
Text: Secular - Andrew Marvell - First was the World as one great Cymbal
                made...
Range: c4-g5, a3-c5, c3-g4, g2-d4
Difficulty: Med Diff

Style: The work opens quietly with a plainsong-like melody introduced by
                unison male voices; this melody recurs in a number of permutations
                throughout the piece. Sectional in a modified point of imitation style.
                Effective use of text painting. Tertian harmonies with minor
                dissonances. Utilizes a mixture of contrapuntal and homophonic
                textures. The effect of the piece is of one long crescendo relieved by
                several quieter thematic statements.

Comments: Divisi writing requires a larger choir. An excellent festival piece and an
                effective setting of this text.

Publisher: Lawson-Gould 51418
Usage: Secular concert
Date: 1969
Level: H.S. - College

145

Composer: Pierce, Brent
Title: How Still He Rests
Voicing: SATB
Accomp: Oboe and wind chimes
Text: Sacred - How still the child rests in quiet splendor
Range: e4-a5, a3-d5, e3-g4, (e2)g2-c4
Difficulty: MED

Style: A contemporary lullaby. The opening section is set for soprano solo;
                mid-section begins with 3-part women and then moves into a 4-part
                homophonic setting; soprano solo returns in final section but is now

accompanied by choir. Wind chimes create interesting atmosphere for the plaintive melody.

Comments: Requires strong soprano soloist. Unusual and intriguing material for Christmas.

Publisher: Walton Music Corp. W2951
Usage: Christmas
Date: 1971
Level: H.S.

146

Composer: Pierce, Brent
Title: Hosanna #2 from JAZZ FRAGMENTS
Voicing: SATB
Accomp: Piano, flute, trumpet, trombone, bass and drums
Text: Secular - Hosanna
Range: f4-a5, c4-e5, d3-g4, d3-d4   Soprano lies a little high
Difficulty: MED

Style: Jazz. Rapidly shifting meter. Short melodic motives are tossed about through the various voices, punctuated by short homophonic exclamations.

Comments: Fun piece for h.s. chorus; accessible for average or better choir. Entire set is good and makes an effective group.

Publisher: Walton Music Corp 2970
Usage: Secular concert or jazz-pop concert
Date: 1974
Level: H.S.

147

Composer: Piket, Frederick
Title: Sea Charm
Voicing: SATB
Accomp: a cappella
Text: Secular poems by Langston Hughes
Range: d4-g#5, a3-f5, b2-g4, f2-e4
Difficulty: Diff

Style: Homophonic settings of ten short poems. Frequent open fifths, bitonality, and sharp dissonances. Effective settings of the texts.; captures the rhythm and spirit of the sea.

Comments: Difficult but accessible to good h.s. chorus. Work may be done in its entirety or may be excerpted. Good exposure to close and dissonant harmonies. Well worth the effort.

Publisher: Associated Music Publishers A-141-29
Duration: 9:
Usage: Secular concert
Date: 1948
Level: H.S. - college

                                   148

Composer: Pinkham, Daniel
Title: A Carol for New Year's Day
Voicing: SATB
Accomp: a cappella
Text: Sacred - Joys secure God's Michael sings. Born to us is Israel's King
Range: f4-g5, b3-d5, c4-a4, g2-b3
Difficulty: Med Dif

Style: Homophonic. In a lively tempo, meter alternates between 6, 9, and 12/8. Tonal, but sharp dissonances occur unexpectedly from added tones. A joyful, dancelike tune.

Comments: Tenor line lies quite high, but work could be done with boys singing in falsetto. Good program material.

Publisher: E.C. Schirmer 2952
Usage: Christmas
Date: 1974
Level: H.S. - college

                                   149

Composer: Pinkham, Daniel
Title: In the Beginning of Creation
Voicing: SATB
Accomp: Electronic tape
Text: Sacred - Genesis 1:1-3
Range: g#3-g5, g#3-d5, g#2-d4, g#2-c4

SATB

Difficulty:	Med Easy
Style:	Avant garde. Mixes pre-recorded electronic sounds with choir singing in a traditional manner as well as whispering, speech, tone clusters, improvisation and glissandi. Basically unison with the exception of tone clusters and the final chord.
Comments:	An excellent introduction to music utilizing electronic tape. Quite accessible to the average h.s. choir. Fine material.
Publisher:	E.C. Schirmer 2902
Duration:	3:08
Usage:	Secular - sacred concert
Date:	1970
Level:	H.S.

150

Composer:	Pinkham, Daniel
Title:	The Sheepheards Song
Voicing:	SATB
Accomp:	Electronic tape
Text:	Sacred - Old English from ENGLAND'S HELICON, 1600
Range:	d4-g5, g3-c5, ab3-g4, g2-c4
Difficulty:	Med Dif
Style:	The tape mirrors the atmosphere of the text. Harmonies are a mixture of traditional writing and sharp dissonances. The tape and chorus alternate until the end of the work when they sound together. Tempo is moderate; many unusual rhythmic devices.
Comments:	Accessible to the average or better h.s. choir. Unusual and interesting material for the Christmas concert. Soprano solo.
Publisher:	Ione Press, Inc. (E.C. Schirmer)
Usage:	Sacred - secular concert - Christmas
Date:	1972
Level:	H.S.

151

Composer:	Pinkham, Daniel
Title:	Piping Anne and Husky Paul
Voicing:	SATB

Accomp:	a cappella
Text:	Secular poem by Robert Hillyer: Piping Anne and husky Paul, once they swelled our madrigal...
Range:	d4-g5, g3-b4, d3-g4, g2-g3
Difficulty:	MED

Style: Alternates between homophonic and soli unison sections. Meter alternates between 9/8 and 12/8. A contemporary madrigal. Added tones add a little mild dissonance. Lively tempo. Light, spirited work.

Comments: Good for either choir or small ensemble. Fine program material for the developing choir.

Publisher:	E.C. Schirmer
Usage:	Secular concert
Date:	1956
Level:	H.S.

152

Composer:	Poulenc, Francis
Title:	Tenebrae factae sunt
Voicing:	SATB
Accomp:	Organ
Text:	Sacred - Latin and English - Darkness was over all
Range:	d4-f#5, b3-e5, f3-g4, g#2-c4
Difficulty:	Med Dif

Style: A slow, calm work featuring extensive use of changing meters. A mixture of contrapuntal and homophonic textures. Harmony is tonal but dissonant with frequent 7th and 9th chords. A well written work effectively expressing the text.

Comments: Typical Poulenc but not overly dissonant. With hard work the piece would be accessible to the average h.s. choir. Soprano solo.

Publisher:	Editions Salabert S.A. Paris
Usage:	Sacred - secular concert
Date:	1961
Level:	H.S. - college

153

Composer:	Powell, Robert

SATB

Title:	What Star is This *
Voicing:	SATB
Accomp:	a cappella
Text:	Sacred text by Charles Coffin
Range:	c#4-f#5, b3-a4, d3-d4, f#2-b3
Difficulty:	Easy

Style: This piece is in 3 sections with the chorus and soloist singing simultaneously in the first and last sections. Tempo is quite slow and in 4/4 throughout. A smoothly flowing, chorale like work.

Comments: A lovely piece. Excellent material for the Christmas concert. Soprano solo.

Publisher:	Carl Fischer, Inc. CM 8018
Usage:	Sacred - secular concert - Christmas
Date:	1977
Level:	H.S.

154

Composer:	Rabe, Folke
Title:	Rondes
Voicing:	SATB
Accomp:	a cappella
Text:	Secular - nonsense syllables - vowels, glottal sounds, etc.
Range:	c4-f#4, c4-f4, c3-a4, d3-c4
Difficulty:	MED

Style: Avant garde. Somewhat tongue-in-cheek treatment of avant garde techniques. Utilizes simultaneous, random staccato pitches, glissandi, flares, siren type sounds, telephone #'s and movement.

Comments: Accessible for most h.s. choirs. Good introduction to avant garde techniques. A crowd pleaser.

Publisher:	Wilhelm Hansen (G. Schirmer) 11894
Usage:	Secular concert
Date:	1967
Level:	H.S. - college

155

Composer:	Rorem, Ned

Title: Three Prayers
Voicing: SATB
Accomp: a cappella
Text: Sacred - 1) Creator Spirit, who dost lightly hover 2) Father, guide and
                lead me 3) Creator Spirit, please
Range: e4-f#5, b3-c5, d3-f#4, f#2-c4
Difficulty: Diff

Style: Homophonic settings. Harmony moves from very traditional to quite
                dissonant. Some unusual progressions. Rhythmically all three settings
                are straightforward with basic movement in eighth- and quarter-note
                figures. #1 is characterized by frequent triplet figures.

Comments: Three short but interesting pieces. Conjunct movement makes the parts
                quite singable. Challenging but accessible to average and better choirs.

Publisher: Boosey & Hawkes 5912
Usage: Sacred - secular concert
Date: 1973
Level: H.S.-college

156

Composer: Rorem, Ned
Title: Three Motets
Voicing: SATB
Accomp: Organ
Text: Sacred - Old English from poems by Gerard Manley Hopkins
Range: c4-g(a)5, g3-f5, c3-(a)f#4, g#2-d4
Difficulty: MED

Style: There are three pieces in this set whose tempi range from moderate to
                very brisk. A mixture of contrapuntal, homophonic, and unison textures
                with frequent melismatic passages. Harmonies alternate between fairly
                traditional writing and sharp dissonances

Comments: A fairly straightforward, but interesting set. May be sung individually or
                as a group.

Publisher: Boosey & Hawkes
Usage: Sacred - secular concert
Date: 1973
Level: H.S. - college

157

Composer:	Ross, M. Keith
Title:	Wrestling Jacob
Voicing:	SATB
Accomp:	Handbells and snare drum
Text:	Sacred - Charles Wesley
Range:	e4-f#5, c#4-c#5, e3-e4, a2-b3
Difficulty:	Med Easy

Style:
The Scottish air that serves as the melody for this Charles Wesley hymn is treated differently in each of the three verses. After a brief introduction by handbells, the melody is presented in the soprano and alto lines over a sparse accompaniment. In the second verse, a dialogue between men's and women's voices is doubled by the handbells. The third verse is an a cappella statement set homophonically. Traditional harmonies with generous use of open fifths.

Comments:
An interesting setting of this hymn tune and text. The bell accompaniment is effective, and the piece is written well for high school voices. Accessible for the church youth choir.

Publisher:	Beckenhorst Press, Inc. HP1304
Usage:	Sacred concert - general anthem
Date:	1988
Level:	H.S.

158

Composer:	Rutter, John
Title:	Seeds Grow to Plants
Voicing:	SATB
Accomp:	Piano
Text:	Secular - Seeds grow to plants if you add a little water.
Range:	d4-f#5, g3-c5, d3-f#4, a2-d4
Difficulty:	Med Easy

Style:
This text is set in a theme and variations form. The tuneful melody is first stated by the sopranos and altos in unison and then followed immediately by the tenors and basses. Both of these verses are sung over an arpeggiated accompaniment. The third verse is contrapuntal, the melody divided between the various voice parts with some divisi writing in the women's voices. The fourth verse is set homophonically except for an imitative treatement of the final phrase.

Comments: A singable and tuneful work, popular for high schools choirs. Good program material.

Publisher: Bourne Co. B234716-357
Usage: Secular concert
Date: 1978
Level: H.S.

159

Composer: Rutter, John
Title: What Sweeter Music
Voicing: SATB
Accomp: organ
Text: Sacred - Robert Herrick
Range: db4-gb5, Bb3-c4, db3-gb4, gb3-eb4
Difficulty: MED

Style: The work is characterized by a smoothly flowing melody line typical of Rutter's compositions. Dialogue between soli sections and full chorus alternating between men's and women's voices. Primarily homophonic. Tonal with mild dissonances resulting from passing tones and added tones. Theme and variations form.

Comments: A tuneful Christmas anthem. This would be a marvelous addition to any Christmas program.

Publisher: Oxford University Press
Usage: Christmas
Date: 1988
Level: H.S.

160

Composer: Rutter, John
Title: O Clap Your Hands
Voicing: SATB
Accomp: Organ
Text: Sacred - Psalm 47:1-7
Range: d4-g5, g#3-eb5, d3-g4, g#2-e4
Difficulty: Med Easy

SATB

Style:
A fanfare anthem. Rhythmic, in a rapid tempo with frequently changing meters. A cantabile middle section contrasts with the more exclamatory outer sections. Some sharp dissonances although the work is quite tonal.

Comments:
An exciting work. Requires a large chorus. This would be a good festival selection.

Publisher: Oxford University Press 42.378
Usage: Sacred - secular concert
Date: 1973
Level: H.S.

161

Composer: Rutter, John
Title: Praise Ye the Lord
Voicing: SATB
Accomp: Organ
Text: Sacred - Psalm 150
Range: d4-g5, d#4-e5, a3-g4, e3-e4
Difficulty: Med Easy

Style:
Work is rhythmic in a lively tempo. Marcato writing sometimes is relieved by a more legato style. Primarily homophonic. Fairly traditional harmonies.

Comments:
An attractive, lively work. Baritone solo.

Publisher: Oxford University Press
Usage: Sacred - secular concert
Date: 1969
Level: H.S.

162

Composer: Rutter, John
Title: Riddle Song
Voicing: SATB
Accomp: Piano
Text: Secular - I have a young sister far beyond the sea; many be the dowries that she sent me...
Range: f4-g5, Bb3-c5, f3-g4, ab2-eb4
Difficulty: Med Easy

Style:	Tonal. Opens with an extended soprano soli. Remainder of work alternates between hymn style treatment of melody and melody with chordal "ah" accompaniment. Quietly moving ballad style.
Comments:	A lovely piece. Quite accessible to most H.S. groups.
Publisher:	Oxford University Press 84-230
Usage:	Secular concert
Date:	1973
Level:	H.S.

163

Composer:	Schickele, Peter
Title:	Three Choruses from e.e. cummings
Voicing:	SATB
Accomp:	a cappella
Text:	Secular poems by e.e. cummings - 1) Dominic Has, 2) Dim/1(a, 3) Maggie and Milly and Molly and May
Range:	c#4-f5, Bb3-eb4, d3-eB4, g2-eb4
Difficulty:	Med Dif
Style:	The first piece is set in a fast tempo, the second in a slow tempo, and the third in a moderate tempo. Some changing meters. Basically homophonic with some contrapuntal sections. Rhythmic. The harmonic approach is contemporary with mild dissonances.
Comments:	These pieces are lighthearted and highly rhythmic. They are most effective when performed as a set. Interesting program material.
Publisher:	Alexander Broude, Inc.
Duration:	3:
Usage:	Secular concert
Date:	1967
Level:	H.S. - college

164

Composer:	Schuman, William
Title:	The Lord Has a Child
Voicing:	SATB
Accomp:	Organ or Piano
Text:	Sacred poem by Langston Hughes
Range:	c4-e5, Bb3-Bb4, d3-e4, g2-c4

Difficulty: Med Dif

Style: Constantly shifting tonal centers. Much of the work is traditional, but
                       the constant modulation makes the piece quite interesting. Homophonic.
                       ABA form.

Comments: Fairly traditional work.

Publisher: Merion Music Inc. (Theodore Presser)
Usage: Secular - sacred concert
Date: 1957
Level: H.S.

165

Composer: Schuman, William
Title: To All, to Each from CAROLS OF DEATH
Voicing: SATB
Accomp: a cappella
Text: Secular text by Walt Whitman
Range: e4-f5, b3-c4, e3-e4, a2-d4
Difficulty: Med Dif

Style: A quiet, slow but intense work. Unusual inversions, with many open
                       octaves that lend a mysterious quality to the work. Mildly dissonant;
                       7ths require careful tuning. Long sustained phrases. Opening is
                       contrapuntal; remainder of work is basically homophonic.

Comments: An excellent piece; requires a mature choir to negotiate the long,
                       sustained phrases.

Publisher: Merion Music, Inc. (Theodore Presser)
Usage: Secular concert
Date: 1959
Level: H.S. - college

166

Composer: Schuman, William
Title: The Last Invocation from CAROLS OF DEATH
Voicing: SATB
Accomp: a cappella
Text: Secular - Walt Whitman
Range: c#4-f#5, Bb3-b4, c#2-e4, ab2-c4

Difficulty: Med Dif

Style: A slow, intense work featuring interesting harmonic devices within a fairly homophonic texture. Unconventional chord structures with frequent use of dissonant intervals. Changing meters. Dynamics require careful attention.

Comments: An intense and effective setting of the text. Requires a mature choir.

Publisher: Merion Music, Inc. 342-40011
Usage: Secular concert
Date: 1959
Level: H.S.

167

Composer: Schuman, William
Title: The Unknown Region from CAROLS OF DEATH
Voicing: SATB
Accomp: a cappella
Text: Secular text by Walt Whitman
Range: f#4-g5, c#4-c5, c#3-f4, g#2-c4
Difficulty: Med Dif

Style: Through-composed. Highly rhythmic throughout with short legato sections breaking the rhythmic intensity. Opens with a chordal ostinato figure which is repeated with variations later in the work. Much of the work is built on 7th and 9th chords in unusual inversions.

Comments: An intense, exciting, rhythmic work. A classic.   Not for the timid. Requires an excellent chorus.

Publisher: Merion Music, Inc. 342-40012
Usage: Secular concert
Date: 1959
Level: H.S. - college

168

Composer: Schuman, William
Title: Thrift #2 of FOUR ROUNDS ON FAMOUS WORDS
Voicing: SATB
Accomp: a cappella
Text: Secular - He that goes a borrowing goes a sorrowing

SATB

Range:	c4-eb5, c4-eb5, c3-eb4, c3-eb4
Difficulty:	Med Easy

Style: Melody is initially stated in unison but tossed between men's and women's voices; canonic treatment follows, resulting in interesting dissonances. Short coda ends the work. Moderate tempo in cut time.

Comments: Good teaching material for the young choir as well as interesting program material.

Publisher:	Merion Music, Inc. 342-40001-4
Usage:	Secular concert
Date:	1957
Level:	H.S.

169

Composer:	Schuman, William
Title:	Health #2 from FOUR ROUNDS ON FAMOUS WORDS
Voicing:	SATB
Accomp:	a cappella
Text:	Secular - Early to bed and early to rise...
Range:	c4-d5, c4-d5, c3-d4, c3-d4
Difficulty:	Easy

Style: Polyphonic. Women sing the melody in unison; then melody is treated canonically. Work ends with a short coda. Tonal in G major.

Comments: All four of these rounds are quite singable and clever. Good program material for young choirs.

Publisher:	Merion Music, Inc. 342-40000
Usage:	Secular concert
Date:	1957
Level:	H.S.

170

Composer:	Seiber, Mátyás
Title:	Three Hungarian Folk-songs
Voicing:	SATB
Accomp:	a cappella
Text:	Secular - 1) The Handsome Butcher; 2) Apple, Apple; 3) The Old Woman

| Range: | c#4-e5, b3-b4, e3-a4, c#3-e4 |
| Difficulty: | Med Easy |

| Style: | Rhythmic folk-song settings. #2 is slower in contrast with the rapid movement of the outer two sections. Homophonic texture. Most dissonances occur as passing tones. |

| Comments: | Standard literature for the h.s. choir. Useful for small ensembles. Good for developing articulation, dynamic sensitivity, and phrasing. |

Publisher:	J. Curwen & Sons Ltd.
Duration:	3:10
Usage:	Secular concert
Date:	1955
Level:	H.S.

171

Composer:	Slater, Richard W.
Title:	Ascribe Unto the Lord *
Voicing:	SATB
Accomp:	Organ and timpani
Text:	Sacred - Psalm 29 - Ascribe unto the Lord, o ye mighty, worship and strength
Range:	d4-a5, c4-d5, d3-g4, f2-d4 Tenor lies a little high
Difficulty:	Diff

| Style: | Highly rhythmic with frequently shifting meters. Opens slowly with a fanfare statement, then moves into major central section characterized by driving rhythmic treatment. Ends with short recapitulation of opening. Conjunct lines make handling of dissonances fairly easy. |

| Comments: | Exciting work for good h.s. choir. |

Publisher:	World Library Pub., Inc. CA-4025
Usage:	Sacred - secular concert
Date:	1977
Level:	H.S. - college

172

Composer:	Smith, Robert Edward
Title:	Where are All Thy Beauties Now
Voicing:	SATB

Accomp:	Piano
Text:	Secular poem by Thomas Campion - Where are all Thy Beauties Now, all hearts enchaining?
Range:	d4-g5, ab3-c5, eb3-eb4, g2-c4
Difficulty:	MED
Style:	Homophonic. Lush harmonies; added tones with frequent supension resolution figures. Short, lyrical, plaintive melody in soprano. Triple meter, tempo di valse. A theme and variations form.
Comments:	A lovely piece for h.s. singers. Good program material.
Publisher:	Continuo Music Press Inc. (Alexander Broude)
Usage:	Secular concert
Date:	1980
Level:	H.S.

173

Composer:	Spencer, Williametta
Title:	Mystic Trumpeter
Voicing:	SATB
Accomp:	a cappella
Text:	Secular - Walt Whitman
Range:	c4-a5, g#3-e5, d3-g4, ab2-f#4
Difficulty:	Med Dif
Style:	Chromatic and dissonant with frequently changing tonal centers. This is a dramatic piece which builds in intensity as it moves to the final cadence. Rhythmic with changing meters. Extensive use of dynamic contrast. The texture is a mixture of contrapuntal and homophonic styles with generous use of paired voices.
Comments:	An effective piece and a good show piece for a strong choir. Although quite dissonant, the dissonances are generally approached by step and can be mastered without great difficulty. Although ranges appear extreme, the tessituras of all voices are good.
Publisher:	National Music Publishers WHC No. 15
Usage:	Secular concert
Date:	1969
Level:	H.S.

174

Composer: Spencer, Williametta
Title: O My Luve's Like a Red, Red Rose
Voicing: SATB
Accomp: a cappella
Text: Secular - Robert Burns
Range: c#4-a5, b3-e5, c#3-f#4, f#2-e4
Difficulty: Med Dif

Style: This short octavo is in ABA form with coda. The texture is primarily contrapuntal with some use of short paired duets. The harmony is tonal, but dissonant with many added tones, passing tones and suspension figures. Part writing is disjunct, particurly in the outer voices. The tempo is slow (eighth note=100), but there is constant rhythmic movement giving a linear flow to the piece.

Comments: The close harmonies make this a challenging piece for many high school choirs; however, it is a satisfying work. It would be good material for a chamber choir as well as a full chorus.

Publisher: National Music Publishers NMP 150
Usage: Secular concert
Date: 1983
Level: H.S. - College

175

Composer: Steinmetz, John
Title: Chorus
Voicing: SATB
Accomp: a cappella
Text: Secular - no text
Range: c4-c5, g3-c4, f3-c4, g2-f3
Difficulty: Med Dif

Style: Avant garde. No apparent tonality, yet frequently resolves at ends of phrases to C major in men's voices and Bb in women's voices. No strict meter. Extensive use of dynamics. Mid-section features slow vocal trills in female voices.

Comments: A good introduction to avant garde techniques. Soprano and alto solos.

Publisher: Plymouth Music Co., Inc.
Usage: Secular concert

SATB

Date: 1978
Level: H.S.

176

Composer: Stevens, Halsey
Title: Winter from SONGS FROM THE PAIUTE, a set of 7 pieces
                     published separately
Voicing: SATB
Accomp: Flutes and timpani
Text: Translations of Paiute Indian poems - The red clouds of sunset are
                     drifting like down on the peaks of the mountains
Range: e4-f#5, b3-b4, e3-c4, a2-g3
Difficulty: Med Easy

Style: Paired duets throughout. Mildly dissonant. Duets move in thirds for the
                     most part. Some quartal harmony when duets sound simultaneously. No
                     rhythmic problems. Long instrumental introduction.

Comments: An interesting set well within the scope of the average h.s. chorus.
                     Good program material. Instrumentation lends new timbres to the
                     typical choral concert.

Publisher: Mark Foster M364A
Duration: 2:24
Usage: Secular concert
Date: 1981
Level: H.S. - college

177

Composer: Stevens, Halsey
Title: Hungarian Folksongs
Voicing: SATB
Accomp: a cappella
Text: Secular
Range: c4-g5, g3-d5, c3-f#4, g2-d4
Difficulty: MED

Style: Three short folksong settings. Tempos vary from moderately fast to very
                     fast. The meter alternates in each of the pieces between 2/4 and 3/4.
                     Much use of two-part writing. Tonal with some fairly sharp dissonances.

Comments: A unique and interesting set of pieces.

Publisher: Marko Press   (Mark Foster Music Co.)
Usage: Secular concert
Date: 1970
Level: H.S.

178

Composer: Stevens, Halsey
Title: Go, Lovely Rose
Voicing: SATB
Accomp: a cappella
Text: Secular poem by Edmund Waller - Go, lovely rose, tell her that wastes
             her time and me
Range: d4-a5, g3-e5, d3-g4, e2-db4
Difficulty: Med Dif

Style: Homophonic. Rich, lush, chordal structure throughout. Frequent meter
             changes. Mild dissonances. Interesting alternation between duple and
             triple rhythmic patterns. Tempo is andante with half note=60.

Comments: A beautiful piece. Requires a mature choir. Ranges are quite wide in all
             voices although the tessituras are generally good.

Publisher: Helios Music Edition
Duration: 1:32
Usage: Secular concert
Date: 1954
Level: H.S. - college

179

Composer: Susa, Conrad
Title: Pretty Polly (No. 2 of TWO BALLADS)
Voicing: SATB
Accomp: Piano
Text: Secular - Appalachian Folk-song
Range: a3-f5, b2-f4
Difficulty: Med Easy

Style: Opens in a rapid tempo [quarter note=138] in duple meter. The piano
             accompaniment effectively captures the changing moods of the ballad
             text. Open fifths are prevalent in the harmonies. The texture is a
             mixture of homophonic and contrapuntal styles.

Comments: This is the second of TWO BALLADS set by Susa, and like the first is characterized by an exciting and demanding piano accompaniment. An interesting and expressive work. Good program material for the young choir.

Publisher: E.C. Schirmer 2931
Usage: Secular concert
Date: 1972
Level: H.S.

180

Composer: Susa, Conrad
Title: Red Rosey Bush (No. 1 of TWO BALLADS)
Voicing: SATB
Accomp: Piano
Text: Secular - Appalachian Folk-song
Range: a3-g5, Bb2-f4
Difficulty: Med Easy

Style: This is a two-voice setting of the familiar ballad. Each of the five verses of text is treated distinctively. The first verse is a homophonic statement of the melody; in the second the basses state the melody alone in a more forceful and syncopated style; the third and fourth verses are contrapuntal and rhythmically complex, and the final verse is in augmentation. All of these occur over a highly developed piano accompaniment. Tonal, but utilizes sharp and surprising dissonances.

Comments: Although this is a two-part work (SB), it is interesting program material. Accessible to a young high school choir, but requires an excellent accompanist.

Publisher: E.C. Schirmer 2930
Usage: Secular concert
Date: 1972
Level: H.S.

181

Composer: Susa, Conrad
Title: The Birds
Voicing: SATB
Accomp: Organ

Text: Sacred poem by Hilaire Belloc - When Jesus Christ was four years old, the angels brought him toys of gold

Range: d4-a5, Bb3-e5, c3-a4, Bb2-e4

Difficulty: Med Dif

Style: Opening section is a dialogue between soli voices and choir. Some use of polytonality. Dissonances are usually approached stepwise. Extensive soli and unison sections in work.

Comments: Difficult accompaniment. Work requires organ. Piano would detract from the overall effectiveness of the piece. A good tenor section is necessary. Lovely piece.

Publisher: E.C. Schirmer 2778

Usage: Sacred - secular concert

Date: 1967

Level: H.S. - college

182

Composer: Tate, Phyllis

Title: Engraved on the Collar of a Dog, which I gave to His Royal Highness

Voicing: SATB

Accomp: a cappella

Text: Secular poem by Alexander Pope

Range: d4-f5, c4-d5, c#3-f#4, g#2-d4

Difficulty: Med Dif

Style: A novelty piece in triple meter. Primarily eighth-note movement; tempo indication is allegro vivace-quasi tarantella. Has howling glissandi in middle section. Ending section includes long triadic melismas on "whose" and ends with a ff woof.

Comments: A cute, but moderately difficult novelty selection that a fairly sophisticated h.s. choir might appreciate.

Publisher: Oxford University Press

Usage: Secular concert

Date: 1976

Level: H.S. - college

183

Composer: Thompson, Randall

Title: Two Worlds

SATB

Voicing:	SATB
Accomp:	Piano
Text:	Secular - Edward Waller - The seas are quiet when the winds give o'er; so calm are we when ...
Range:	Bb3-a5, g3-d#5, Bb3-g#5, e2-d4
Difficulty:	MED

Style: The piano accompaniment contributes significantly to the interest of this work. Triplet figures are predominant throughout, creating an undulating movement over which the voice parts are laid. Movement in the voice parts is principally in quarter and half notes. As is typical of much of Thompson's writing, the work builds to a large climax which is followed by a short, quiet ending statement.

Comments: Requires a large and/or mature high school choir. A good accompanist is necessary for a successful performance of this work.

Publisher:	E.C. Schirmer 3041
Usage:	Secular concert
Date:	1978
Level:	H.S. - College

184

Composer:	Thompson, Randall
Title:	The Happy Shore
Voicing:	SATB
Accomp:	Piano or strings
Text:	Secular - Edmund Spenser
Range:	d4-b5, a3-d5, d3-a4, g2-e4
Difficulty:	Diff

Style: The work opens quietly somewhat in the style of a chorale with short instrumental interjections. Extensive use of short sequential phrases. Rapid movement through tonal centers builds tension. The dynamic, harmonic, and rhythmic structures intensify to an extended climax followed by a short, quiet vocal statement and final piano ending.

Comments: This is vintage Thompson, but as always is fine material. Requires a larger and more mature high school choir. This would be good festival material. Although the vocal ranges are quite wide, the tessituras of all voices are suitable for h.s.

Publisher:	E.C. Schirmer 3053

Usage: Secular concert
Date: 1980
Level: H.S. - College

185

Composer: Thompson, Randall
Title: The Light of Stars
Voicing: SATB
Accomp: a cappella
Text: Secular - Henry Wadsworth Longfellow
Range: d4-b5, g3-e5, d3-a4, f#2-e4
Difficulty: Med Dif

Style: The texture is primarily contrapuntal throughout with constant harmonic movement typical of Thompson's writing. Mildly dissonant. The tempo is slow with rhythmic movement principally in quarter- and half-note figures. The piece begins quietly and builds slowly to a fortissimo climax before a quiet decrescendo to the end.

Comments: Requires a mature high school choir because of both the extensive ranges of the voice parts and the long, sustained, unaccompanied vocal lines. An excellent piece for a festival or a strong high school choir.

Publisher: E.C. Schirmer 2554
Usage: Secular concert
Date: 1980
Level: H.S.- College

186

Composer: Thompson, Randall
Title: Choose Something Like a Star   from FROSTIANA
Voicing: SATB
Accomp: Piano
Text: Secular poem by Robert Frost
Range: b3-g5, g3-c5, d3-g4, g2-d4
Difficulty: Med Dif

Style: Homophonic throughout. Voices move in long, sustained phrases over an ostinato figure in piano accompaniment. Parallel chords are used frequently. Work begins very quietly and gradually builds in intensity.

Comments: A classic, often performed, but still a majestic piece.

SATB

Publisher: E.C. Schirmer #2487
Usage: Secular concert
Date: 1959
Level: H.S. - college

187

Composer: Thompson, Randall
Title: The Road not Taken   from FROSTIANA
Voicing: SATB
Accomp: Piano
Text: Secular poem by Robert Frost
Range: a3-f5, f3-d5, c3-f4, d2-d4
Difficulty: Med Dif

Style: Homophonic throughout. Sounds almost strophic, but each new verse
                 has a subtle harmonic variation. 1st two verses are in unison. March-like
                 tempo. In minor mode with lowered 7th.

Comments: Another often performed work by Thompson. An important part of the
                 literature. Fairly extreme ranges in bass and alto lines.

Publisher: E.C. Schirmer #2485
Usage: Secular concert
Date: 1959
Level: H.S. - college

188

Composer: Thompson, Randall
Title: The Best of Rooms
Voicing: SATB
Accomp: a cappella
Text: Sacred - Christ, He requires still, wheresoe'er He comes
Range: c4-a5, ab3-eb5, d3-f#4, gb2-c4
Difficulty: Diff

Style: Typical Thompson. Mixture of homophonic and contrapuntal styles.
                 Frequent use of paired duets. The slow beginning gives way to more
                 rapidly moving central section characterized by eighth-note melismas;
                 closes quitly and slowly.

Comments: Requires a good h.s. chorus. As always, well worth the effort.

Publisher: E.C. Schirmer #2672
Usage: Sacred - secular concert
Date: 1963
Level: H.S. - college

189

Composer: Thompson, Randall
Title: Glory to God in the Highest
Voicing: SATB
Accomp: a cappella
Text: Sacred - Luke 2, 14
Range: c4-g5, g3-e5, e3-a4, g2-d4
Difficulty: Med Dif

Style: In ABA form; the outer sections are homophonic and rhythmic with frequently shifting meters. Mid-section is slower, contrapuntal, and a 3-part setting for bass, tenor, and alto. Traditional harmonies.

Comments: A standard repertoire selection for the h.s. choir.

Publisher: E.C. Schirmer 2470
Usage: Sacred - secular
Date: 1958
Level: H.S. - college

190

Composer: Thompson, Randall
Title: The Paper Reeds by the Brooks   from THE PEACEABLE KINGDOM
Voicing: SATB
Accomp: a cappella
Text: Sacred - Isaiah 19:7
Range: b3-f#5, f#3-b4, e3-g4, e2-d4
Difficulty: MED

Style: A legato work with smoothly flowing lines in an adagio throughout. A mixture of homophonic and contrapuntal textures. Harmonies are fairly traditional.

Comments: A readily accessible work. Excellent for developing expressive singing and sensitivity to phrasing.

SATB

Publisher: E.C. Schirmer
Usage: Sacred - secular concert
Date: 1936
Level: H.S.

191

Composer: Thompson, Randall
Title: Alleluia
Voicing: SATB
Accomp: a cappella
Text: Sacred - Alleluia
Range: b3-a5, a3-d5, d3-a4, f#2(d2)-d4
Difficulty: Med Dif

Style: A slow, majestic reiteration of the exclamation "Alleluia." Primarily
                    contrapuntal with extended melismatic passages. Harmonies are fairly
                    traditional with frequent use of 3rds and 6ths. The piece builds to a
                    climax, followed by an ending denouement.

Comments: Another Thompson classic. Often performed but still a marvelous
                    work. Extremely difficult to maintain intonation and intensity
                    throughout the work. Not for the beginning choir.

Publisher: E.C. Schirmer
Usage: Sacred - secular concert
Date: 1940
Level: H.S. - college

192

Composer: Thompson, Randall
Title: The Last Words of David
Voicing: SATB
Accomp: Piano
Text: Sacred - II Samuel, XVIII:3-4 - He that ruleth over men must be just
Range: d4-a5, b3-c4, b2-c4, g2-e4
Difficulty: Med Dif

Style: Characteristically, this piece opens homophonically and then moves into
                    a longer contrapuntal section with running melismas in the individual
                    parts. Very dramatic; ff opening gives way to the quieter alleluia and
                    amen.

Comments:	A classic, but not for the average h.s. choir. Only a large, mature h.s. choir should attempt this. Good festival music, frequently performed.
Publisher:	E.C. Schirmer 2294
Usage:	Sacred - secular concert
Date:	1950
Level:	H.S. - college

193

Composer:	Thybo, Leif
Title:	Bees
Voicing:	SATB
Accomp:	a cappella
Text:	Secular
Range:	c#4-g5, b3-e5, c#3-g4, a2-c#4
Difficulty:	MED

Style:	A rhythmic piece in a moderate tempo with a preponderance of eighth-note and triplet figures. Basically homophonic with a rapidly changing harmonic rhythm. Contemporary harmonies with frequent use of 2nds but no extreme dissonances.
Comments:	A nonsensical, lighthearted piece accessible to the average h.s. chorus.
Publisher:	Walton Music Corp.
Usage:	Secular concert
Date:	1978
Level:	H.S.

194

Composer:	Toch, Ernst
Title:	Geographical Fugue
Voicing:	SATB (Speech chorus)
Accomp:	a cappella
Text:	Secular - Names of countries and cities rhythmically combined
Range:	
Difficulty:	MED

Style:	A speech chorus treated as a four-voice fugue. No pitch notation is used, only rhythms.

SATB

Comments: An excellent teaching tool, as well as providing different and interesting program material.

Publisher: Mills Music Inc.
Usage: Secular concert
Date: 1930
Level: H.S. - jr. high

195

Composer: Trubitt, Allen R.
Title: Three Songs on the Shortness of Life *
Voicing: SATB
Accomp: a cappella
Text: Secular - 1) Injurious Hours, 2) Life is a Poet's Fable, 3) Our Hasty Life
Range: db4-g5, g3-d5, c#3-g4, (e2)g2-d4
Difficulty: Med Dif

Style: The pieces employ a mixture of homophonic and contrapuntal textures. A non-traditional approach to harmony is evident throughout; tonal centers shift frequently. Added tones create mild dissonances. Frequent meter changes but rhythms are not problematic.

Comments: An interesting and well written set of pieces accessible to the average h.s. choir.

Publisher: Roger Dean Pub. Co.
Duration: 6:30
Usage: Secular concert
Date: 1973
Level: H.S.

196

Composer: Vaughan Williams, Ralph
Title: Fain Would I Change That Note
Voicing: SATB
Accomp: a cappella
Text: Secular - Fain would I change that note to which fond love hath charmed me.

Range: c4-d5, b3-Bb4, f3-f4, f2-Bb3
Difficulty: Med Easy

Style: Traditional harmonies throughout. The basic texture is homophonic. Rhythmic movement is principally in quarter and half notes. The meter alternates between triple and duple time in a moderate tempo. The form is a two-part strophic construction.

Comments: Good material for blending and balancing a young high school chorus. The harmony is traditional with mild dissonances resulting from passing tone movement. This piece would work well with a small ensemble.

Publisher: Novello & Co., Ltd. 1030
Usage: Secular concert
Date: 1907
Level: H.S.

197

Composer: Walter, Samuel
Title: Thou Hidden Love of God *
Voicing: SATB
Accomp: a cappella
Text: Sacred
Range: eb4-f5, d4-b4, g3-f4, ab2-c4
Difficulty: Med Easy

Style: A simple, short piece set in a moderate 4/4. Alternates between contrapuntal and homophonic textures. Harmonies are mainly traditional with some use of contemporary, non-traditional techniques.

Comments: A sensitive setting of the text. Quite accessible to most h.s. choirs.

Publisher: Abingdon Press
Usage: Sacred - secular concert
Date: 1975
Level: H.S.

198

Composer: Walton, William
Title: What Cheer?
Voicing: SATB
Accomp: a cappella

SATB

Text:	Sacred (A Christmas Carol) from Richard Hill
Range:	f#4-g5, a3-f#5, d2-f#4, b2-d4
Difficulty:	MED

Style: A lively, bouncing piece in 3/8 meter. Homophonic throughout. Harmonies are fairly traditional. Syncopation is used frequently adding to the rhythmic appeal of the work. Basically a strophic piece with variations.

Comments: An attractive work that would be good program material for any Christmas concert. Accessible to most h.s. choirs.

Publisher:	Oxford University Press
Usage:	Secular concert - Christmas
Date:	1961
Level:	H.S. - college

199

Composer:	Washburn, Robert
Title:	Voyager's Song from THREE THOUGHTS FROM THOREAU
Voicing:	SATB
Accomp:	Piano
Text:	Secular - Gentle river, swiftly glides thy stream along many a bold adventurous voyage.
Range:	d4-g5, c4-f5, a2-f4, g2-f4
Difficulty:	Med Dif

Style: This piece moves rapidly [eighth note = 220] in meters alternating between 7/8, 6/8, and 9/8 time. The mild dissonances are punctuated by consonant cadences throughout. Paired and simultaneous duets are used extensively.

Comments: The wide ranges in the three lower voices may discourage wide performance of this work by high school choruses; nevertheless, if the individual voice lines are learned melodically, this would be a delightful concert piece.

Publisher:	Boosey & Hawkes 6086
Duration:	1:40
Usage:	Secular concert
Date:	1982
Level:	H.S. - College

200

Composer:	Washburn, Robert
Title:	Now Welcome Summer
Voicing:	SATB
Accomp:	Piano
Text:	Secular - Now welcome summer with gladness and mirth.
Range:	c4-g5, g3-c5, d3-g4, f2-f4
Difficulty:	Med Dif

Style: This contemporary madrigal is in theme and variations form. It is in a brisk tempo, rhythmic, and has frequently changing meters. The melodic line is primarily conjunct, and the majority of the harmonies are traditional and tonal, but rather dissonant The verses alternate between a cappella and accompanied treatment; texture is primarily homophonic.

Comments: An appealing and lively work. This piece would work well with a chamber choir or madrigal group.

Publisher:	Oxford University Press 95.202
Usage:	Secular concert
Date:	1967
Level:	H.S.

201

Composer:	Welin, Karl-Erik
Title:	Four Chinese Poems
Voicing:	SATB
Accomp:	a cappella
Text:	Secular
Range:	d#4-g#5, Bb3-c#5, db3-g4, a2-b3
Difficulty:	Med Dif

Style: Four short, pensive, mood pieces, each set in a medium tempo. Basically contrapuntal; mildly dissonant. Several artificial scales are used giving the pieces an oriental quality. Cadences are generally in tertian harmony. Effective settings of the texts

Comments: These pieces are short and skillfully written. Interesting and accessible program material.

Publisher:	Walton Music Corp
Usage:	Secular concert
Date:	1978

SATB

Level: H.S.

                                202

Composer: Wetzler, Robert
Title: Laughing Song
Voicing: SATB
Accomp: a cappella
Text: Secular - William Blake
Range: d4-g5, a3-e5, d3-f#4, g2-d4
Difficulty: Med Easy

Style: This is a short, brisk and delightful setting of Blake's text.
                         Through-composed with the various short sections utilizing unison,
                         canonic and homophonic textures. Tertian harmonies. Voice parts are
                         primarily conjunct. There are no rhythmic problems

Comments: Good program material for a young high school choir. Even though
                         this is a short work, it would be useful in developing phrasing and
                         sensitivity to line in the young choir.

Publisher: Curtis House of Music   C8823
Duration: 1:00
Usage: Secular Concert
Date: 1988
Level: H.S.

                                203

Composer: White, Louise L.
Title: Saint Teresa's Book Mark
Voicing: SATB
Accomp: a cappella
Text: Sacred text by Saint Teresa of Avila (1575-1582) - Let nothing disturb
                         thee, nothing affright thee..
Range: eb4-eb5, c4-c5, g3-g4, g2-c4
Difficulty: MED

Style: A short, quiet and sensitive setting of a beautiful text. Each phrase of
                         the text is set independently; in the two outer sections the soprano line
                         is set in opposition to the lower three voices. The two interior
                         statements are set imitatively in paired duets. Mildly dissonant.

Comments: An effective piece. Requires sustained and controlled singing. Part of the tenor line lies a little high in the voice, but a good falsetto technique would handle the part easily.

Publisher: E.C. Schirmer ECS No. 3140
Usage: Sacred-secular concert
Date: 1982
Level: H.S. - College

204

Composer:	Benjamin, Thomas
Title:	Laudate Dominum
Voicing:	SATB Divisi
Accomp:	a cappella
Text:	Sacred - Latin
Range:	Bb3-Bb5, f#3-c5, d3-f4, g2(e2)-c4
Difficulty:	Diff

Style: A brisk and rhythmic piece employing both homophonic and contrapuntal textures. Harmonies are fairly traditional, but mildly dissonant. Frequent changing meters. Quite a lot of syncopation. There is limited use of speech chant.

Comments: An interesting work with colorful harmonies. Requires a strong h.s. choir.

Publisher:	Fostco Music Press (Mark Foster Music Co.) MF142
Usage:	Sacred - secular concert
Date:	1975
Level:	H.S.

205

Composer:	Boyajian, Gloria
Title:	Let the Whole Creation Cry Glory *
Voicing:	SATB (occasional divisi)
Accomp:	Organ - 2 trumpets, 2 horns & 1 trombone
Text:	Sacred
Range:	e4-a5, b3-d5, e3-f#4, (e)g2-c#4
Difficulty:	Med Easy

Style: Alternating homophonic and contrapuntal textures. The piece begins in a lively tempo; much rhythmic variety with frequent use of syncopation. Solo voices are featured in the slower, more subdued mid-section. Original material returns in the final section. Changing meter throughout.

Comments: An effective and well written piece enhanced by the use of the brass accompaniment. Requires strong baritone and soprano soloists.

Publisher: World Library Pub., Inc.

Usage: Sacred - secular concert
Date: 1975
Level: H.S. - college

206

Composer: Bright, Houston
Title: The Stars are with the Voyager
Voicing: SATB (Soprano and Bass divisi)
Accomp: a cappella
Text: Secular poem by Thomas Hood
Range: d4-a5, a3-c5, d3-f4, e2(d2)-c4
Difficulty: MED

Style: Alternates between a smoothly flowing legato style in 6/8 and a slower mid-section with changing meters. Outer sections are characterized by a very singable, conjunct melody. Basically tertian harmony with some added tones.

Comments: A well written and effective work.

Publisher: Shawnee Press, Inc.
Duration: 3:00
Usage: Secular concert
Date: 1959
Level: H.S.

207

Composer: Britten, Benjamin
Title: A Hymn to the Virgin
Voicing: SATB - SATB
Accomp: a cappella
Text: Sacred - Mixture of Latin and English - Of one that is so fair and bright. Velut maris stella
Range: e4-g5, a3-e5, e3-g4, a2-d4
Difficulty: Med Dif

Style: Homophonic dialogue between the two choirs. Modal; opens in 8, middle section is in a very slow 4. Short Latin responses somewhat like a litany.

Comments: Chorus II may be performed by a solo quartet. Good Christmas material.

Publisher: Boosey & Hawkes - 1856

Usage:	Christmas
Date:	1935
Level:	H.S. - college

208

Composer:	Butler, Eugene
Title:	Late Have I Loved Thee
Voicing:	SSATBB
Accomp:	a cappella
Text:	Sacred text by St. Augustine
Range:	d4-g5, d4-e5, d3-f#4, g2-c4
Difficulty:	MED

Style: This piece opens in a slow tempo, moves to a faster central section, then returns to the opening tempo. Mixed meters include 5/4, 4/4, and 3/4. Both homophonic and contrapuntal textures are used. Harmonies are primarily traditional with some use of added tones.

Comments: An effective work featuring full, rich sonorities.

Publisher:	W-7 Music Corp. (Warner Bros. Publications Inc.)
Usage:	Sacred - secular concert
Date:	1969
Level:	H.S.

209

Composer:	Carter, John
Title:	The Last Invocation *
Voicing:	SSATB
Accomp:	a cappella
Text:	Secular poem by Walt Whitman - At the last tenderly, from the walls of the powerful fortress
Range:	d4-g5, c4-c5, d3-e4, f2-c4
Difficulty:	Med Dif

Style: Basically homophonic. Close dissonances abound, but short unison sections help keep tonal center secure. Triplets and two-against-three rhythms are frequent. Moderate tempo. Legato style.

Comments: A challenging work but worth the effort for the strong h.s. choir or small ensemble.

Publisher:	Edward B. Marks MC4626
Duration:	2:15
Usage:	Secular concert
Date:	1975
Level:	H.S. - college

210

Composer:	Casals, Pablo
Title:	O Vos Omnes
Voicing:	SATB-Divisi
Accomp:	a cappella
Text:	Sacred
Range:	d4-Bb5, Bb3-cb5, eb3-cb4, f2-eb4
Difficulty:	MED

Style: Sustained and expressive with wide dynamic variation. Tertian harmonies with some chromatic movement; effective use of suspension figures. The texture is principally homophonic. There are several instances of alternation between the lower voices and tutti chorus. The tempo is quite slow (lento) with movement primarily in quarter notes.

Comments: A classic; this work calls for sensitive singing and careful attention to phrasing. It requires a great deal of breath control. Not particularly difficult rhythmically or harmonically.

Publisher:	Tetra Music Corp. TC128
Duration:	3:00
Usage:	Sacred - Secular concert
Date:	1965
Level:	H.S. - College

211

Composer:	Clausen, René
Title:	All That Hath Life and Breath Praise Ye the Lord
Voicing:	SATB - Divisi
Accomp:	a cappella
Text:	Sacred - Psalms 96 & 22
Range:	d4-a5, a3-d5, g3-f4, d3-d4
Difficulty:	Med Diff

Style: Sectional in a modified ritornello style. A mixture of contrapuntal and homophonic textures. Tonal, but utilizes parallel chords, tone clusters and added tones. One section incorporates short melodic fragments randomly repeated and superimposed on each other. Rhythmic, moving in a lilting tempo with quarter note = 78 in 6/8 meter.

Comments: This piece belongs in the standard repertoire for both high school and church choirs. A lively and exciting work accessible to high school singers. A good introduction to twentieth-century compositional techniques in the '70's. Some divisi in all parts.

Publisher: Fostco Music Press MF223
Usage: Sacred - secular concert
Date: 1981
Level: H.S. - College

                                  212

Composer: Copland, Aaron
Title: The Promise of Living   from THE TENDER LAND
Voicing: SATBB
Accomp: Piano (four hands)
Text: Secular
Range: c4-f(Bb)5, Bb3-d(f)5, c3-f(Bb)4, g2-d(f)4
Difficulty: MED

Style: A gently flowing piece with frequently changing meters. A mixture of unison, homophonic and contrapuntal textures. Fairly traditional harmonies with frequent use of 2nds and 9ths. Long sustained phrases. ABA form. Closes with a big, triumphant finale.

Comments: This is festival material. Ranges are extreme. Requires excellent accompanists.

Publisher: Boosey & Hawkes 5020
Usage: Secular concert - Festival
Date: 1954
Level: H.S. - college

                                  213

Composer: Felciano, Richard
Title: Words of St. Peter *
Voicing: SAATB
Accomp: Organ and electronic tape
Text: Sacred - I Peter 2:1-9 - Come to him, to that living stone

Range: d4-g5, g3-e5, e3-a4, b2-c#4
Difficulty: Diff

Style: Avant garde, non tonal, sharp dissonances. The tape does not enter
                    until ending of piece. Moderate tempo. Mixture of homophonic and
                    contrapuntal writing.

Comments: An effective piece that is accessible to a h.s. chorus with good readers.
                    Traditional notation and singing style.

Publisher: World Library Pub. Inc CA-2093-8
Usage: Sacred-secular concert
Date: 1970
Level: H.S. - college

214

Composer: Ferris, William
Title: Modern Music
Voicing: SATB - Divisi
Accomp: Piano or orchestra
Text: Secular - William Billings - We are met for a concert of modern
                    invention. To tickle the ear is...
Range: e4-g#5, g3-e5, d3-g#4, a2-e4
Difficulty: Diff

Style: Tonal but dissonant; extensive use of 2nds and 7ths and some quartal
                    harmonies. There are several rapidly moving melismatic sections in the
                    work. A mixture of homophonic and contrapuntal textures with one
                    extended fugal section. The accompaniment is often in dialogue with
                    voices and complements the vocal writing. Frequent tempo and meter
                    changes.

Comments: A clever and effective setting of this Billings text. A difficult work, but
                    one that would be particularly rewarding for a talented festival chorus.
                    Requires a strong accompanist.

Publisher: Oxford University Press
Duration: 10:00
Usage: Festival - Secular concert
Date: 1989
Level: H.S. - College

215

Composer:	Fetler, Paul
Title:	Make a Joyful Noise
Voicing:	SATB (occasional divisi in alto)
Accomp:	a cappella
Text:	Sacred - Psalm 66:1,2,4
Range:	d4-ab5, a3-e5, d3-g44, a2-d4
Difficulty:	Med Dif

Style: A rhythmic piece employing frequent changing meters. The beginning and ending sections are marcato contrasting with the slower and more legato mid-section. Mildly dissonant with an abundance of major 2nds.

Comments: An exciting and effective work. Well suited to the voice. Requires a reasonably strong choir.

Publisher:	Augsburg Publishing House
Usage:	Sacred - secular concert
Date:	1966
Level:	H.S. - college

216

Composer:	Fetler, Paul
Title:	Sing Unto God
Voicing:	SSAATBB
Accomp:	a cappella
Text:	Sacred - Psalm 68:32, 33, 34
Range:	eb4-g5, c4-Bb4, eb3-eb4, ab2-c4
Difficulty:	Med Dif

Style: Rhythmic fanfare anthem. Shifting meters and syncopation. ABA form; the middle section is somewhat quieter than the driving outer sections. A good bit of voice doubling produces rich sonorities.

Comments: Accessible to a strong h.s. choir. Exciting, rhythmic piece. Good closer and/or contest material.

Publisher:	Augsburg Publishing Co 1244
Usage:	Sacred - secular concert
Date:	1959
Level:	H.S.

217

Composer:	Fine, Irving
Title:	Have You Seen the White Lily Grow? #2 from THE HOUR GLASS
Voicing:	SATB (extensive divisi)
Accomp:	a cappella
Text:	Secular text by Ben Jonson
Range:	c4-a5, g3-e5, e3-f#4, e2-e4
Difficulty:	Med Dif

Style: This piece is set in a moderate tempo alternating between 4/4 and 2/4. The divisi writing and extensive use of added tones result in rich sonorities. Primarily homophonic with tertian harmonies.

Comments: An expressive work but requires a strong choral ensemble.

Publisher:	G. Schirmer, Inc.
Usage:	Secular concert
Date:	1951
Level:	H.S.

218

Composer:	Fissinger, Edwin
Title:	Arise, Shine, For Thy Light Is Come
Voicing:	SATB Divisi
Accomp:	a cappella
Text:	Sacred - Isaiah 60:1-2
Range:	c4-ab5, ab3-f5, c3-ab4, f2-f4
Difficulty:	Med Dif

Style: The work opens and closes with a rhythmic and rapidly moving fanfare statement. Rhythmic throughout with frequently changing meters. Tonal but dissonant. The central section of the piece is slower and utilizes much divisi writing. Homophonic.

Comments: An exciting and challenging work. Good material for a mature h.s. chorus or for a festival choir. Wide ranges, but the extremes occur in divisi sections.

Publisher:	Jenson Publications, Inc. 411-01024
Usage:	Festival-sacred-secular concert
Date:	1981
Level:	H.S.

219

Composer:	Fissinger, Edwin
Title:	Make Haste, O God
Voicing:	SATB - divisi
Accomp:	a cappella
Text:	Sacred - Psalm 70: 1,4
Range:	eb4-ab5, Bb3-d5, c3-f4, ab3-eb4
Difficulty:	MED

Style: In ABA form; the A section is built on short declamatory statements. The B section begins with a point of imitation before moving to a climactic chordal statement of "God, be magnificent." Sharp dissonances with liberal use of added tones. Rhythmic in a moderately fast tempo [quarter note=96].

Comments: An exciting work accessible to a strong h.s. choir. Most of the divisi writing is in the soprano and tenor lines.

Publisher:	Walton Music Corp. - WW1086
Usage:	Sacred - secular concert
Date:	1987
Level:	H.S. - college

220

Composer:	Fissinger, Edwin
Title:	Welcome Yule
Voicing:	SSAATBB tenor and soprano soli
Accomp:	a cappella
Text:	Secular - Christmas - Welcome yule, thou merry man, in worship of this holy day
Range:	e4-a5, ab3-eb5, eb3-f4, f2-eb4
Difficulty:	Med Dif

Style: A joyful, rhythmic Christmas carol. Many simultaneously sounding paired duets. Mixture of homophonic and contrapuntal textures. Frequently changing meters. Dissonant, but clearly has tonal center.

Comments: Exciting new Christmas carol. Good work for a mature h.s. choir.

Publisher:	Jenson Pub., Inc. 411-23024
Usage:	Christmas
Date:	1980
Level:	H.S. - college:

221

Composer:	Fissinger, Edwin
Title:	Clap Your Hands *
Voicing:	SSAATTBB
Accomp:	a cappella
Text:	Sacred - Psalms 47, 34, 28
Range:	d4-Bb5, c4-f5, c3-g4, g2-e4 1st soprano lies a little high
Difficulty:	Diff

Style: Opens with fast rhythmic treatment; moves into slower central section and accelerates to a triumphant finale. Sharp dissonances. Individual lines are basically characterized by conjunct movement. Generally homophonic throughout.

Comments: Exciting work accessible to mature h.s. choir.

Publisher:	Jenson Pub., Inc. 411-03014
Usage:	Sacred - secular concert
Date:	1980
Level:	H.S. - college

222

Composer:	Fissinger, Edwin
Title:	By the Waters of Babylon
Voicing:	SSAATTBB
Accomp:	a cappella
Text:	Sacred - Psalm 137 - By the waters of Babylon, there we sat down and wept
Range:	c4-Bb5, ab3-eb5, c3-g4, a2-e4 1st sop is quite high
Difficulty:	Diff

Style: Combines speech chorus and narrator with traditional choral singing. Harsh dissonances contrast with lush chords in a tonal harmonic treatment. Primarily homophonic with short contrapuntal sections. ABA form.

Comments: An effective and exciting work. Very demanding. Is accessible to large, mature h.s. chorus. Good festival material.

Publisher:	Walton Music Corp 2935
Usage:	Sacred - secular concert - Festival
Date:	1977
Level:	H.S. - college

223

Composer:	Fissinger, Edwin
Title:	Make We Joy
Voicing:	SSATB
Accomp:	Handbells, tambourine, drum
Text:	Sacred
Range:	d4-f5, b3-e5, c3-e4, f2-e4
Difficulty:	Med Easy

Style: In a moderately slow tempo that remains constant throughout. Tenors and basses have a repetitive figure of perfect 5ths through much of the piece, contrasting with sections of unison singing. Soprano and alto parts feature extensive use of 3rds and 5ths.

Comments: Handbells, tambourine and drum contribute to the overall effectiveness of this work. A fairly accessible and interesting piece.

Publisher:	Walton Music Corp
Usage:	Sacred - secular concert - Christmas
Date:	1978
Level:	H.S.

224

Composer:	Fritschel, James
Title:	Be Still
Voicing:	SATB frequent divisi in all parts
Accomp:	a cappella
Text:	Sacred - Psalm 46:10
Range:	d4-ab5, g3-f5, g2-f5, g2-c#4
Difficulty:	Diff

Style: The work is set in a moderate tempo and features several contemporary techniques including unmeasured trills, sharp dissonances and novel uses of dynamics (ppp-fff). Basically contrapuntal. Mid-section is bi-tonal. Frequently changing meters and unusual rhythmic groupings.

Comments: A difficult but effective work requiring a fairly large group for successful performance.

Publisher:	Walton Music Corp 2920
Usage:	Sacred - secular concert
Date:	1974
Level:	H.S. - college

225

Composer:	Fritschel, James
Title:	In Peace and Joy
Voicing:	SATB (frequent divisi)
Accomp:	a cappella
Text:	Sacred text by Martin Luther - In peace and joy, I now depart
Range:	d4-a5, a3-d5, e3-f#4(g4), e2(d2)-b3 bass voice lies quite low
Difficulty:	MED

Style: A legato piece employing both homophonic and contrapuntal textures. Few tempo and meter changes. Added tones and divisi writing provide rich sonorities. Major and minor 2nds are prevalent.

Comments: Requires a fairly large and mature chorus because of the frequent divisi writing.

Publisher:	Augsburg Publishing House 11-1755
Usage:	Sacred - secular concert
Date:	1975
Level:	H.S. - college

226

Composer:	Fritschel, James
Title:	My Heart Dances
Voicing:	SATB - divisi
Accomp:	a cappella
Text:	Sacred - Psalm 28
Range:	b3-Bb5, g#3-e5, b3-a4, e2-g4
Difficulty:	Diff

Style: Highly rhythmic and contrapuntal. Sharp dissonances but accessible harmonies. Point of imitation style. Several choral ostinato figures established in the lower three voices with free melodic treatment superimposed in the soprano voice. A moving tone cluster is established in the central section of the work by having each voice part repeat a melodic fragment at random. Open fifths and parallel chordal movement.

Comments: This work is not for everyone! Extreme ranges, especially in the lower registers, make it inaccessible to most h.s. choirs, but the baritones and tenors can move up into the next voice part in lower ranges. Would be exciting for an exceptional choir.

Publisher:	Hal Leonard Publishing Corp. - 08610575

Usage: Sacred - concert
Date: 1979
Level: H.S. - College

227

Composer: Harris, Robert A.
Title: Canticle: The Hungry Angels
Voicing: SATB occasional divisi in soprano
Accomp: Organ
Text: Sacred poem by Philip White
Range: d4-g(a)5, a#3-e5, (c#)e3-g4, (e)g2-e4
Difficulty: Med Dif

Style: The outer sections of this work are in a slow tempo; the mid-section moves at a slightly quicker pace. Frequently changing meters. Tonality shifts between tertian harmonies and more dissonant chords. Basically homophonic with short contrapuntal passages.

Comments: A contemplative piece. Through-composed. Requires much attention to phrasing and expression.

Publisher: Mark Foster Music Co. MF 191
Usage: Sacred - secular concert
Date: 1979
Level: H.S.

228

Composer: Hennagin, Michael
Title: Walking on the Green Grass
Voicing: SATTBB
Accomp: a cappella
Text: Secular - American folk-song - Walking on the green grass, walking side by side
Range: d4-g#5, c#4-eb5, b3-f4, Bb2-db4
Difficulty: Med Dif

Style: Rhythmic with changing meters. Basses and tenors establish a syncopated, ostinato figure while sopranos and altos carry the primary melodic material. Mildly dissonant.

Comments: A really fun piece that is now pretty standard repertoire. Requires a strong soprano section. Accessible to the average or better h.s. choir.

Publisher: Boosey & Hawkes 5443
Usage: Secular concert
Date: 1962
Level: H.S. - college

229

Composer: Hillert, Richard
Title: God Has Gone Up with a Shout!   Alleluia!
Voicing: SATB - divisi
Accomp: a cappella
Text: Sacred - Psalm 47: 1,2,5,6,7
Range: c4-f5, a3-c#5, e3-f4, f2-c4
Difficulty: MED

Style: Homophonic. Moves rapidly [quarter note=200] with frequently changing meters. Traditional harmonies with mild dissonances. Sectional, in a modified rondo style. Broad dynamic range.

Comments: A stirring Psalm fanfare. This is good material for a well balanced h.s. choir.

Publisher: Concordia Publishing House - 98-2744
Usage: Sacred, secular concert
Date: 1987
Level: H.S.

230

Composer: Hovland, Egil
Title: Saul
Voicing: SSATBB and Narrator
Accomp: Organ
Text: Sacred - Acts 8:1-4, 7 & 9:1-4 And on that day a great persecution arose against the church in Jerusalem.
Range: e4-g5, g3-e5, e3-g4, g2-e4 Soprano and tenor lie quite high
Difficulty: Diff

Style: Avant garde. Speech song, improvisation and traditional singing. Sharp dissonances result from chromaticism and added tones. Unison singing and canonic writing are used with triadic cadences.

Comments: A very exciting piece. Requires a fairly large and mature choir. The work is demanding but is not as difficult as it appears.

Publisher: Walton Music Corp M-126
Usage: Sacred - secular concert
Date: 1972
Level: H.S. - college

231

Composer: Ives, Charles
Title: The Sixty-Seventh Psalm
Voicing: SSAATTBB
Accomp: a cappella
Text: Sacred - Psalm 67 - God be merciful unto us and bless us
Range: f4-gb5, c4-f5, c#3-g4, g2-a3
Difficulty: Diff

Style: Polytonal. Homophonic. Opens with mf statement, moves into middle fanfare section characterized by triplet movement, and concludes with choral chant.

Comments: Vintage Ives. A classic. This piece is too difficult for the average h.s. choir, but would make a great festival piece.

Publisher: Associated Music Pub. A-274
Usage: Sacred - secular concert - Festival
Date: 1939
Level: College - H.S. festival

232

Composer: Ives, Charles
Title: Circus Band
Voicing: SATB - Divisi
Accomp: Piano - four hands
Text: Secular
Range: c4-a5, c4-f5, c3-a4, f2-f4
Difficulty: MED

Style: The majority of this delightful piece is in unison; the final verse is set for six-part divisi choir and is quite contrapuntal. The entire work is rhythmic with extensive use of syncopation and cross accents. The four-hand piano accompaniment requires two strong accompanists. The melodic lines are primarily conjunct with some chromaticism.

Comments: A fun piece. Good material for an American group on a concert program. Excellent introduction to Ives and to twentieth-century music.

Publisher: Peer International Corp.
Usage: Secular concert
Date: 1973
Level: H.S. - College

233

Composer: Kraehenbuehl, David
Title: Ideo gloria in excelsis Deo *
Voicing: SSATBB
Accomp: a cappella
Text: Sacred - English & Latin - On this day earth shall ring with the song children sing...
Range: c4-g5, f3-Bb4, c3-d4, g2-c4 Alto lies quite low in voice
Difficulty: Med Dif

Style: Through-composed with each verse of text scored for different combinations of voices. Rhythmic with marcato pulse; extensive syncopation and rhythmic displacement. Tonal. Added tones and passing tones result in mild dissonances.

Comments: Requires a strong alto section. 1st tenors could double altos. Rhythmically exciting work.

Publisher: Associated Music Pub. A-193
Usage: Christmas
Date: 1954
Level: H.S. - college

234

Composer: Larsen, Libby
Title: . . . And Sparrows Everywhere
Voicing: SATB - divisi
Accomp: a cappella
Text: Secular - Keith Gunderson
Range: c4-g5, c4-c5, d3-g4, g3-c4
Difficulty: Med Diff

Style:	This is a set of three short pieces: 1) Chameleon Wedding; 2) Snails; 3) Hawks and Sparrows and Sparrows. Nos. 1 and 3 are contrapuntal with paired duets and imitative treatment. No. 2 introduces an alto solo over an ostinato humming accompaniment. Tonal, but liberally laced with dissonances. Effective use of text painting. The set presents no rhythmic difficulties. Contrasting tempos among the three in keeping with the nature of each text. 1) presto; 2) slowly; 3) moderately.
Comments:	A delightful set that should have great appeal for h.s. singers. Challenging but accessible. The texts are whimsical nature poems.
Publisher:	E. C. Schirmer - E.C.S. No. 3106
Duration:	3:15
Usage:	Secular concert
Date:	1985
Level:	H.S. - college

235

Composer:	Lovelock, William
Title:	Death Carol from WHEN LILACS LAST IN THE DOORYARD BLOOMED *
Voicing:	SATB divisi and solos in all pts
Accomp:	a cappella
Text:	Secular text by Walt Whitman
Range:	C#-b5, a3-e5, c3-a4, (d)f2-e4 occasional high tess in sop & ten.
Difficulty:	Dif
Style:	A sectional piece utilizing a mixture of contrapuntal and homophonic textures. Two soloists are required from each section. Harmonies are contemporary but tonal; major 7th chords are common.
Comments:	A lengthy and difficult work, but interesting music. Good festival material.
Publisher:	Walton Music Corp 2975
Duration:	5:45
Usage:	Secular concert - Festival
Date:	1975
Level:	H.S. - college

236

Composer:	Luboff, Norman
Title:	Gloria Patri
Voicing:	SSATTB
Accomp:	a cappella
Text:	Sacred
Range:	e4-g5, Bb3-Bb4, Bb2-g4, eb3-Bb4
Difficulty:	MED

Style: A rather short and somewhat static setting of the Gloria Patri. Basically a dialogue between men's and women's voices. Alternating sections sustain a unison pedal tone while the other voices move chordally. Dissonant but not strident. In a moderate 4 with quarter-note movement predominant.

Comments: A simple and effective setting of a familiar text. Good church material. Long sustained lines.

Publisher:	Walton Music Corp. 3058
Usage:	Sacred - secular concert
Date:	1972
Level:	H.S.

237

Composer:	Mathew, David
Title:	Identity
Voicing:	Mixed speaking chorus for 16 voices
Accomp:	a cappella
Text:	The name of each speaker
Range:	
Difficulty:	Easy

Style: Speaking chorus. Moves from solo entrances to full chorus. A lot of dynamic inflection, giving wave-like effect to the work.

Comments: Easy. Good introduction to novel usage of the speaking voice in avant garde music.

Publisher:	Oxford University Press
Duration:	3:30
Usage:	Secular concert
Date:	1972
Level:	H.S. - jr. high

238

Composer:	Mathias, William
Title:	Let the People Praise Thee, O God
Voicing:	SATB - divisi
Accomp:	Organ
Text:	Sacred - Psalm 67
Range:	c#4-ab5, ab3-eb5, eb3-ab4, g3-d4
Difficulty:	Med Dif

Style: This anthem is in modified ritornello form in a lively 6/8 meter. The ritornello section is a dancelike setting of the text "Let the people praise Thee, O God." A central soprano soli section moves in a smooth legato style, providing contrast with the more rhythmic outer sections. The intermediate sections are rhythmic, characterized by 2 against 3 figurations. Major and minor 2nds are common in the divisi writing adding dissonance to an overall consonant harmony.

Comments: An exciting work. Accompaniment is intended for organ, but would work with piano.

Publisher:	Oxford University Press - A331
Usage:	Sacred - secular concert
Date:	1981
Level:	H.S. - college

239

Composer:	Mechem, Kirke
Title:	Dan-U-EL
Voicing:	SATB - divisi - baritone solo
Accomp:	piano
Text:	A mixture of sacred and secular texts
Range:	c4-a5, ab3-d5, d3-a4
Difficulty:	Med Diff

Style: An exciting and dramatic work based on the story of John Brown, the Civil War abolitionist. In the style of a Negro spiritual, highly rhythmic. Continuous dialogue between the baritone soloist and the choir. Different ostinato figures are established throughout the piece. Heavily syncopated and rhythmic accompaniment.

Comments: Calls for a strong, mature baritone soloist. The solo's tessitura is high with numerous e's and f's. This is an excellent festival piece and accessible to an excellent h.s. choir. Requires a strong accompanist.

Publisher:	G. Schirmer - 12596
Duration:	5:30
Usage:	Festival
Date:	1986
Level:	H.S. - College

240

Composer:	Moe, Daniel
Title:	A Babe is Born
Voicing:	SATB (Some divisi in soprano line)
Accomp:	a cappella
Text:	Sacred
Range:	d4-f5, g3-Bb4, eb3-g4, g2-c4
Difficulty:	MED

Style: Homophonic; contrapuntal and unison textures are employed. Harmonies are fairly contemporary with extensive use of 7ths and 9ths. Legato style in 6/8 meter.

Comments: An interesting work for the Christmas program. Parts lie well in the voices.

Publisher:	Theodore Presser Co.
Usage:	Sacred - secular concert - Christmas
Date:	1955
Level:	H.S.

241

Composer:	Moe, Daniel
Title:	Fall Softly, Snow *
Voicing:	SATB - Soprano solo (occasional divisi in sop)
Accomp:	a cappella
Text:	Sacred - Fall softly snow on the scarred earth
Range:	c#4-g5(ab5), g#3-c5, d#3-f4, f2-db4
Difficulty:	Med Dif

Style: A slow, legato work with a short contrasting mid-section in a faster tempo. Disjunct melodic line in soprano solo. Contrapuntal; tonal, but utilizes some sharp dissonances. Frequent meter changes.

Comments: A fairly difficult work but worth the effort.

Publisher:	Augsburg Publishing House 11-0510
Usage:	Christmas
Date:	1963
Level:	H.S. - college

242

Composer:	Nin-Culmell, Joaquin
Title:	Three Traditional Cuban Songs
Voicing:	SATB - Divisi
Accomp:	a cappella
Text:	Secular 1) The Lost Child 2) Come Here for Your Fruit Pulp 3) Where is the Ma Teodora?
Range:	eb4-a5, g3-db4, c3-ab4, f2-c4
Difficulty:	Med Diff

Style:	All three settings are tonal with a distinctive Spanish flavor. Frequent dissonances resulting from passing tones and added tones. The rhythms in the second two songs are characterized by triplet figures and cross and shifting accents and meters. A mixture of homophonic and contrapuntal textures. In the second song, three separate melodic lines are sung simultaneously over a bass pedal tone.
Comments:	Difficult but delightful pieces. Rather extreme ranges in the the tenor voice require a more mature group of singers or judicious use of falsetto. Excellent material for an advanced high school choir.

Publisher:	Rongwen Music, Inc.
Usage:	Secular concert
Date:	1983
Level:	H.S. - College

243

Composer:	Nystedt, Knut
Title:	O Crux
Voicing:	SSAATTBB
Accomp:	a cappella
Text:	Sacred - Latin - O crux splendidior cunctis astris mundo celebris (O Cross, more radiant than the earth...)
Range:	c#4-a6, g3-d5, b2-f#4, d2-d4
Difficulty:	Diff

Style:	Dissonant with some use of tone clusters. Nystedt builds cluster figures in two voices in either ascending or descending movement, then introduces a more melodic statement in the other two voices over this texture. Extremely dissonant textures resolve to consonant cadences. Changing meters are used to enhance text underlay. The tempo is slow and there are no rhythmic problems. The work opens pianissimo but builds to a fortissimo climax before closing with a pianissimo statement.
Comments:	A difficult and demanding work suitable for festival use. The ranges are quite broad in the soprano, alto and bass lines. An exciting work, but requires a large chorus. Not a beginning piece.
Publisher:	Hinshaw Music Inc. HMC-286
Usage:	Sacred concert - Anthem for Holy Week
Date:	1978
Level:	H.S. - college

244

Composer:	Nystedt, Knut
Title:	Lamentations of Jeremiah
Voicing:	SATB - divisi
Accomp:	a cappella
Text:	Sacred - Lamentations 1:20-31; 3:40, 55-61; 5:19-22
Range:	c#4-ab5, g#3-eb5, c#3-g4, f#3-eb4
Difficulty:	Diff
Style:	Sectional and episodic. Extremely dissonant with close harmonies and some polytonality. Dramatic with frequently changing tempi and dynamics. Contrapuntal. Opens with alternating cries from the sopranos and altos in open fourths and fifths. Basses and tenors enter with text. Some use of imitation and paired duets.
Comments:	A dramatic piece requiring a mature choir. Extreme ranges in all voices; divisi writing in all parts. Not for everyone, but this could be a most exciting and rewarding work for those choirs that can handle it.
Publisher:	Augsburg Publishing House - 11-4504
Duration:	5:45
Usage:	Sacred - secular concert
Date:	1987
Level:	H.S. - college

245

Composer:	Nystedt, Knut
Title:	I Will Praise Thee, O Lord
Voicing:	SSATB
Accomp:	a cappella
Text:	Sacred - Psalm 9:2
Range:	g4-g5, e4-d5, b3-f#4, a2-d4
Difficulty:	MED

Style: ABA form; the two outer sections are homophonic and are in a fanfare setting. Middle section is a short fugal section. Tonal, some use of added tones. Inversions create frequent open fourths between soprano and alto lines, adding to the fanfare quality.

Comments: Requires good soprano section. Good contest material. Predates the Nystedt tone clusters.

Publisher:	Augsburg Publishing House
Usage:	Secular - sacred concert
Date:	1958
Level:	H.S. - college

246

Composer:	Nystedt, Knut
Title:	If you Receive My Words *
Voicing:	SATTBB
Accomp:	a cappella
Text:	Sacred - Proverbs 2:1-15, 3:1-4
Range:	b3-g5, b3-d5, b2-f#4, g2-d4
Difficulty:	Diff

Style: Avant garde. Moving tone clusters and some solo recitation. The piece makes frequent use of 2nds and other dissonant intervals as well as unisons and more consonant harmonies. Traditional choral sections are homophonic and utilize a good bit of bitonality. Tempi range from slow to moderately fast.

Comments: This works requires a strong chorus and an especially strong men's section.

Publisher:	Augsburg Publishing House 11-9214
Usage:	Sacred - secular concert
Date:	1973

Level: H.S. - college

247

Composer: Nystedt, Knut
Title: I Will be as the Dew *
Voicing: SSATTB
Accomp: a cappella
Text: Sacred - Hosea 14:5-7
Range: d4-f#5, a3-b4, f#3-f#4, d3-c#4
Difficulty: MED

Style: Throughout much of the piece the sopranos and altos sing block chords
                   above a contrasting triplet motive in the tenor and bass lines. Extensive
                   use of 3rds and 4ths. The slower mid-section features some bitonality,
                   but the work is only mildly dissonant

Comments: An effective work. The piece is well within the grasp of the average h.s.
                   choir. Interesting material.

Publisher: Augsburg Publishing House 11-1266
Usage: Sacred - secular concert
Date: 1960
Level: H.S.

248

Composer: Nystedt, Knut
Title: Kyrie   from A THANKSGIVING MASS
Voicing: SSA/SATB Double chorus
Accomp: a cappella
Text: Sacred   - Latin text from the Liturgy
Range: c4-g5, g3-c5, ab2-g4, ab2-eb4
Difficulty: MED

Style: In chant style; unmetered. Many minor 2nds and major 7ths are used.
                   Treble choir alternates with mixed choir and sometimes joins the mixed
                   choir. An interesting setting of this familiar text. Quite dissonant, yet
                   very singable.

Comments: A challenging work but not overly difficult.

Publisher: Walton Music Corp. 2972
Usage: Sacred - secular concert

Date: 1974
Level: H.S.

249

Composer: Page, Robert
Title: Quem vidistis pastores from THREE CHRISTMAS MOTETS
Voicing: SSA - SATB - TBB
Accomp: a cappella
Text: Sacred
Range: a3-g#5, g#3-c#5, eb3-a4, e2-f4   Fairly extreme ranges in sop & bass
Difficulty: Diff

Style: Frequent tempo and meter changes. Quite dissonant. Alternation
             between legato passages and more rhythmic marcato sections. Both
             homophonic and contrapuntal textures are employed. Three ensembles
             are needed for performance. These SSA, SATB, and TTB sections
             alternate throughout the work with occasional simultaneous sounding of
             all three ensembles.

Comments: An interesting work but requires a strong choral ensemble for a
             successful performance. Only a large and quite advanced h.s. choir
             should attempt this piece.

Publisher: Standard Music Publishing, Inc.
Usage: Sacred concert - Christmas and/or festival
Date: 1971
Level: H.S. - college

250

Composer: Persichetti, Vincent
Title: A Clear Midnight   from CELEBRATIONS
Voicing: SATB (Some divisi)
Accomp: Wind ensemble or piano
Text: Secular poem by Walt Whitman
Range: d4-f5, d4-Bb4, d3-f4, c3-Bb3
Difficulty: MED

Style: This piece is set in a slow 3/2 meter. Much tertian harmony is used with
             rich and somewhat dissonant chords. A short, subdued work.

Comments: A short, colorful work requiring careful tuning.

Publisher: Elkan-Vogel, Inc.
Usage: Secular concert
Date: 1967
Level: H.S.

251

Composer: Pierce, Brent
Title: Travelog
Voicing: Mixed Voices (SA TB SATB)
Accomp: Piano, Percussion, Flute
Text: Secular - No text, only vowels and consonant sounds
Range: Utilizes three voices all well within h.s. ranges
Difficulty: Med Easy

Style: Avant garde (mildly). Utilizes stylized melodic material to capture the
               spirit of 1) The American desert; 2) Alaska; 3) India; 4) Israel; 5)
               Japan; 6) Africa. Glottal stops, tongue clicks, improvisation and other
               non-tonal sounds help to create atmospheres expressive of each country
               or region.

Comments: Introduces avant garde sounds and includes suggested choralography.
               Interesting and unusual program material.

Publisher: Walton Music Corp. 2924
Usage: Secular concert
Date: 1976
Level: H.S.

252

Composer: Poorman, Sonja
Title: Sing We and Dance
Voicing: SATB Divisi
Accomp: a cappella
Text: Secular - Sing we now and Dance!
Range: d4-f#5, c#4-d5, e3-g4, a2-c4
Difficulty: Med

Style: Mild dissonances result from frequent passing tones and added tones in
               an otherwise traditional harmonic setting. Rhythmic, in a lively tempo.
               The texture is a mixture of homophonic and contrapuntal styles.

Comments: A relatively easy and accessible piece, suitable for either a small ensemble or large chorus.

Publisher: Galleria Press   GP-106
Usage: Secular concert
Date: 1984
Level: H.S.

253

Composer: Poulenc, Francis
Title: Timor et tremor
Voicing: SSAATBB
Accomp: a cappella
Text: Sacred - Latin - Great fear and trembling have taken hold on me
Range: d#4-g#5, a3-c#5, e3-g#4, g2-f#4
Difficulty: Diff

Style: Homophonic. Dissonant but more accessible than many of Poulenc's motets. Chromatic; through-composed. Primarily quarter-note movement.

Comments: A difficult work but accessible for mature h.s. choirs. Would be a good introduction to Poulenc.

Publisher: Editions Salabert   E.A.S. 16767
Duration: 3:
Usage: Sacred - secular concert - Lent
Date: 1939
Level: H.S. - college

254

Composer: Rickard, Jeffrey H.
Title: Gloria
Voicing: SATB (SSAATTBB)
Accomp: a cappella
Text: Sacred - Latin
Range: eb4-gb5(ab5), Bb3-c5, f3-f4(ab4), f2-eb4
Difficulty: Med Dif

Style: Opens in a fast tempo, moves through a slower mid-section, and returns to the original tempo. Accented, energetic style alternates with slower, more legato passages. Fairly traditional harmonies; employs both homophonic and contrapuntal textures.

Comments: A lively, energetic piece useful as an opener or finale on a Christmas program.

Publisher: Augsburg Pub House
Usage: Christmas
Date: 1971
Level: H.S.

255

Composer: Riegger, Wallingford
Title: Who Can Revoke
Voicing: SSAATTBB
Accomp: Piano
Text: Secular - Who can revoke the axe's stroke that split the heart of living oak?
Range: d4-b5,b3-e5, c3-f#4, Bb2-e4
Difficulty: Diff

Style: An intense and rapidly moving work characterized by a driving piano accompaniment. The vocal writing is primarily diatonic with occasional large leaps. Frequently changing meters. Alternation between men's and women's voices. Texture is primarily homophonic.

Comments: This piece requires an outstanding accompanist. It should be used primarily as a festival piece at the high school level. An exciting work.

Publisher: Edward B. Marks Music
Usage: Festival
Date: 1949
Level: H.S. - College

256

Composer: Rutter, John
Title: Blow, Blow, Thou Winter Wind
Voicing: SATB (Soprano divisi)
Accomp: Piano (accomp for 2 flutes, harpsichord & strings)
Text: Secular - Shakespeare from As You Like It
Range: c4-f5, b3-ab4, c3-f5, g2-db4

Difficulty:	MED
Style:	A smoothly flowing piece in 3/4 meter. Minor with occasional cadences in major. Fairly traditional harmonies with frequent use of suspensions and major 7th chords creating a lush effect. Primarily homophonic with some contrapuntal passages. A lovely, expressive melody runs throughout.
Comments:	A beautiful, expressive work. The added instrumentation provides an especially attractive accompaniment for the piece. Good program material.
Publisher:	Oxford University Press
Usage:	Secular concert
Date:	1975
Level:	H.S.

257

Composer:	Rutter, John
Title:	Open Thou Mine Eyes
Voicing:	SSATBB - Soprano solo
Accomp:	a cappella
Text:	Sacred - Lancelot Andrewes
Range:	c4-f5, a3-a4, c3-f4, f2-d4
Difficulty:	MED
Style:	A melodic piece with mild dissonances, mostly in the form of passing tones. The melody is introduced by a soprano soloist and then passed through a number of variations featuring SSA, TB, SATB, and finally soprano solo again over a four-part humming chorus.
Comments:	A beautiful, flowing work requiring sustained singing. Good material for a mature high school chorus.
Publisher:	Hinshaw Music Inc. HMC-467
Usage:	Sacred concert
Date:	1980
Level:	H.S.

258

Composer:	Rutter, John
Title:	It was a Lover and his Lass
Voicing:	SATBB

Accomp:	a cappella
Text:	Secular - Shakespeare
Range:	d4-g5, b3-c#5, d3-a4, f2-e4
Difficulty:	Med Dif

Style: Jazz setting of a familiar Shakespearian text. Sectional. Opening section sets melody in soprano against "doo-ba-doo" accompaniment in other voices. Middle section is homophonic followed by a recapitulation and coda.

Comments: Fun, but not easy setting; accessible to the average or better h.s. choir.

Publisher:	Oxford University Press 84.255
Usage:	Secular concert
Date:	1975
Level:	H.S.

259

Composer:	Spencer, Williametta
Title:	At the Round Earth's Imagined Corners
Voicing:	SATTBB
Accomp:	a cappella
Text:	Sacred poem by John Donne: At the round earth's imagin'd corners, blow your trumpets, angels, and arise...
Range:	d4-g5, a3-e5, d3-g4, g2-e4
Difficulty:	MED

Style: Rhythmic piece with frequent meter changes. Utilizes frequent open 4ths and 5ths along with added tones. A festive work. Features paired duets which appear between homophonic choral statements.

Comments: Now an old favorite, but excellent program material. Most effective with a fairly large choir.

Publisher:	Shawnee Press, Inc.
Duration:	2:30
Usage:	Sacred - secular concert
Date:	1968
Level:	H.S.

260

Composer:	Stevens, Halsey
Title:	Sung for the Passing of a Beautiful Woman from SONGS FROM THE PAIUTE, a set of 7 pieces published separately
Voicing:	SSATTB
Accomp:	a cappella
Text:	Translations of Paiute Indian poems - Go thy way in comeliness.
Range:	eb4-a5, a3-e5, e3-e4, a2-eb4 1st soprano lies a little high
Difficulty:	MED

Style: Contrapuntal utilizing several paired duets. Mildly dissonant; frequent use of parallel 7ths. Lyrical work. Moderate tempo.

Comments: A lovely piece accessible to average or better h.s. choirs. A number of tuning problems are present requiring good concentration.

Publisher:	Mark Foster MF3646
Duration:	1:24
Usage:	Secular concert
Date:	1981
Level:	H.S. - college

261

Composer:	Stevens, Halsey
Title:	Like as the Culver on the Bared Bough
Voicing:	SSATB
Accomp:	a cappella
Text:	Secular poem by Edmund Spenser - Like as the culver on the bared bough, sits mourning for the absence of her mate.
Range:	c4-g5, g3-a4, d3-g4, f2-e4
Difficulty:	Med Dif

Style: Homophonic. Some alternation between men's and women's trios. Quiet, pensive work. Tonal; utilizes added tones, and frequent passing tones result in mild dissonances. Changing meters and rhythmic groupings add interest to basic eighth- and quarter-note movement.

Comments: Suitable for either small ensemble or full choir.

Publisher:	Associated Music Publishers A-218
Duration:	2:05
Usage:	Secular concert
Date:	1954

Level: H.S. - college

                          262

Composer: Stevens, Halsey
Title: Psalm 117: O Praise the Lord, All Ye Nations
Voicing: SSATBB
Accomp: a cappella
Text: Sacred
Range: f#4-a5, d4-d5, f#3-a4, c#3-d#4
Difficulty: MED

Style: The piece is in an allegro tempo and alternates between 3/4 and 4/4.
                          Much tertian harmony. Homophonic. Some bitonal effects are achieved
                          at times. A festive work. Limited use of hemiola and cross accents.
                          Quite dissonant.

Comments: A good festival piece. Work is best suited for a larger chorus.
                          Interesting material.

Publisher: Mark Foster Music Co. EH-12
Usage: Sacred - secular concert - Festival
Date: 1976
Level: H.S.

                          263

Composer: Thompson, Randall
Title: Ye Were Sometimes Darkness   from REQUIEM
Voicing: SATB/SATB Double chorus
Accomp: a cappella
Text: Sacred
Range: c4-g(a)5, (f)g3-d5, c3-f#(a)4, f2-db4
Difficulty: MED

Style: Work is in 4/4 and opens in a slow tempo. Mid-section is faster.
                          Quarter- and eighth-note movement predominates producing smooth,
                          legato passages throughout. Mildly dissonant. A mixture of homophonic
                          and contrapuntal textures.

Comments: A good work for a large chorus. Not a really demanding work.

Publisher: E.C. Schirmer 2640
Usage: Sacred - secular

Date: 1963
Level: H.S. - college

264

Composer: Track, Gerhard
Title: Sing to God
Voicing: SATB   divisi in Soprano, alto, and tenor
Accomp: a cappella
Text: Sacred - Psalm 68:4
Range: c4-g5, ab3-d5, e3-d4, (eb)f2-Bb3
Difficulty: Med Dif

Style: Changing meters. Highly rhythmic in an andante tempo. A mixture of
                    homophonic and contrapuntal textures. Harmonic effects are fairly
                    contemporary with mild dissonances. Basically work is in ABA form
                    with a quieter, contrapuntal central section that builds to the return of
                    the opening material.

Comments: An exciting, festive work that requires a fairly large, solid chorus.

Publisher: Neil A. Kjos 5942
Usage: Sacred - secular concert
Date: 1977
Level: H.S.

265

Composer: Vaughan Williams, Ralph
Title: Come Away, Death
Voicing: SSATB
Accomp: a cappella
Text: Secular text by Shakespeare
Range: b3-g5, a3-d5, e3-g5, (e)f#2-d4
Difficulty: MED

Style: This piece is set in a slow tempo with unchanging meter. Contrapuntal.
                    Basically conjunct writing in the voice parts. Harmonies are fairly
                    traditional. Expressive phrasing.

Comments: An excellent piece; good material for the chamber choir.

Publisher: Stainer & Bell (Galaxy Music Co.)
Usage: Secular concert
Date: 1909
Level: H.S.

266

Composer:	Vaughan Williams, Ralph
Title:	Nothing is Here for Tears
Voicing:	SATB - Unison
Accomp:	Piano or organ
Text:	Secular - Nothing is here for tears, nothing to wail
Range:	c4-g5, c4-e5, c3-g4, c3-e4
Difficulty:	Easy

Style: Unison choral song with four-part ending. Rich chordal movement in accompaniment is typical of Vaughan Williams. Stately melody and accompaniment. Only the last 12 bars are set for mixed chorus.

Comments: Good unison piece for young chorus.

Publisher:	Oxford University Press OCS1103
Usage:	Secular concert - funeral or memorial service
Date:	1936
Level:	H.S.

267

Composer:	Vick, Lloyd
Title:	Two Choral Fanfares
Voicing:	SATB divisi in all parts
Accomp:	Piano
Text:	Secular - vocal syllables - no text
Range:	e4-g5, b3-d5, e3-f#4, (e)f#2-eb4
Difficulty:	Diff

Style: A set of two choral fanfares. Frequently changing tempi with a variety of rhythmic effects consisting largely of 8th, 16th, and triplet figures. Much use of tertian harmonies. The ah vowel is used throughout.

Comments: A difficult work requiring skill in executing the various rhythmic and melodic motives. Requires a large chorus; interesting festival material.

Publisher:	Walton Music Corp. 2933
Usage:	Secular concert - Festival
Date:	1977
Level:	H.S. - college

268

Composer:	Willcocks, David (arr.)
Title:	Barbara Allen
Voicing:	SAATBB
Accomp:	a cappella
Text:	Secular - The familiar ballad
Range:	eb4-ab5, Bb3-eb5, eb3-g4, eb2(ab2)-eb4
Difficulty:	Med Easy

Style: Vs. 1 is unison; 2 is SSA; 3 and 5 are ATBB; 4 and 6 are SAATBB. Basically homophonic setting with interesting part writing; tonal with mild dissonances resulting from passing tones.

Comments: A beautiful, fresh setting of this familiar ballad. Requires a good soprano section although 1sts can handle high tones while 2nds sing the 1st alto part.

Publisher:	Oxford University Press 53-097
Usage:	Secular concert
Date:	1975
Level:	H.S.

269

Composer:	Zaimont, Judith Lang
Title:	Sunny Airs and Sober (A Book of Madrigals)
Voicing:	SSATB - Soprano, alto, and tenor solos
Accomp:	a cappella
Text:	Secular - Shakespeare, Shelley, Gay and Herrick
Range:	c4-ab5, a3-eb(f#)5, d3-g#4, f2-e4
Difficulty:	Med Dif

Style: The pieces are mildly dissonant, often cadencing on tertian chords. Frequent meter changes. Mixture of homophonic and contrapuntal textures.

Comments: An interesting set of contemporary madrigals; well suited to the voices. May be done individually or as a group. Requires a fairly mature choir.

Publisher:	Walton Music Corp M-144
Usage:	Secular concert
Date:	1977
Level:	H.S. - college

270

Composer:	Christopherson, Dorothy
Title:	My Heart is Ready
Voicing:	SAB
Accomp:	Piano and Percussion
Text:	Sacred - Psalm 108:1,3
Range:	c4-e5, c4-e5, c3-e4
Difficulty:	Med Easy

Style:	Rhythmic with considerable use of syncopated figures. The harmony is quite traditional with mild dissonances. The use of percussion gives the piece a somewhat 'popular' feel. In ABA form with coda.
Comments:	An excellent piece for a high school church youth choir. Very singable; tastefully written.
Publisher:	Augsburg Publishing House 11-4661
Usage:	Sacred - general
Date:	1988
Level:	H.S. - church

271

Composer:	Crocker, Emily
Title:	Rejoice, Alleluia
Voicing:	SAB
Accomp:	a cappella (optional piano part)
Text:	Sacred - I will rejoice in the Lord
Range:	f4-d5, b3-c5, f3-d4
Difficulty:	Easy

Style:	In a lilting 6/8, this is a joyous anthem setting. The basic texture is homophonic, but there is some dialogue between the bass line and the upper two voices. Tertian harmonies.
Comments:	This anthem would work well with a young high school choir or with a junior high chorus. The baritone and alto lines lie well within the ranges of young baritones and boys' changing voices.
Publisher:	Jenson Publications, Inc. 471-18010
Usage:	Sacred-secular concert
Date:	1985
Level:	H.S. - Jr. High

272

Composer:	Dietterich, Philip R.
Title:	O Love That Triumphs Over Loss
Voicing:	SAB
Accomp:	a cappella
Text:	Sacred - Lord Christ, when first you came to earth, upon a cross they bound you.
Range:	c4-f5, a3-d5, c3-d4
Difficulty:	Med Easy

Style: This anthem opens with a unison soli for male voices after which the two upper voices enter over an extended pedal tone. Open fifths and parallel movement characterize the first half of the piece, while the harmonies in the second half are more consonant and traditional. Dietterich has given careful attention to text painting in this short anthem setting.

Comments: Good material for a church youth choir, particularly during the Lenten season.

Publisher:	Sacred Music Press S-301
Usage:	Sacred concert - Lenten anthem
Date:	1983
Level:	H.S.

273

Composer:	Distler, Hugo
Title:	As the Deer Crieth
Voicing:	SAB
Accomp:	a cappella
Text:	Sacred - Psalm 42:1,2
Range:	d4-d5, b3-c5, c3-d4
Difficulty:	MED

Style: A mixture of contrapuntal and homophonic styles. Mildly dissonant with some quartal harmonies. The anthem is in ABA form, the legato B section contrasting with the more rhythmic outer sections. Frequent meter changes.

Comments: A moderately challenging work for high school choirs, but well worth the effort. Stressing of the independent vocal lines is essential to a successful performance.

Publisher: Augsburg Publishing House 11-4612
Usage: Sacred concert - anthem
Date: 1985
Level: H.S. - college

274

Composer: Distler, Hugo
Title: Maria Walks Amid the Thorn
Voicing: SAB
Accomp: a cappella
Text: Sacred - Medieval German Carol
Range: b3-f5, Bb3-b4, Bb2-d4
Difficulty: Med Easy

Style: A very simple but beautiful setting of this unusual carol. Contrapuntal. Although there is a great deal of changing meter in this work, it is not difficult rhythmically. Flowing melodic line.

Comments: This is a short motet, a highly accessible Distler work. Good material for any choir.

Publisher: Concordia Publishing House 98-2306
Usage: Sacred - Christmas
Date: 1968
Level: H.S.

275

Composer: Distler, Hugo
Title: Lord, Keep us Steadfast
Voicing: SAB
Accomp: a cappella
Text: Sacred
Range: f4-f5, g3-Bb4, c3-d4
Difficulty: Med

Style: Contrapuntal. Frequently changing meters. A hymn-anthem setting in ABA form; mid-section is set for two-part women's voices. The independence of the vocal lines makes this a challenging but interesting work.

Comments: Typical Distler. Readily accessible. Good material for a young
                 developing choir.

Publisher: Augsburg Publishing House 11-1448
Usage: Sacred - secular concert
Level: H.S.

276

Composer: Distler, Hugo
Title: For God So Loved the World
Voicing: SAB
Accomp: a cappella
Text: Sacred - John 3:16
Range: d4-f5, g3-c5, c3-c4
Difficulty: Med Easy

Style: Features canonic treatment throughout the work. Frequent use of paired
                 duets in short melismatic sections. Rhythmic displacement is typical of
                 other Distler works. Mildly dissonant.

Comments: An interesting and challenging setting of a familiar text. Challenging
                 material for the young choir.

Publisher: Concordia Pub. House 98-2239
Usage: Sacred concert
Date: 1968
Level: H.S.

277

Composer: Hageman, Philip
Title: De Gustibus
Voicing: SAB
Accomp: Piano
Text: Secular-Of all the Latin I ever heard, I remember this the best: De
                 gustibus non disputandum est.
Range: c4-g5, gb3-c#5,c3-g4
Difficulty: MED

Style: A parody of different musical styles. Sectional with changing meters,
                 tempi, dynamics, keys, etc. Tonal but somewhat dissonant, particularly

in the accompaniment. The refrain "de gustibus" appears at the end of each section, but each time in a new variation.

Comments: This is a clever piece and a wonderful teaching tool. It was composed for a junior high setting, but would work with young high school singers.

Publisher: Oxford University Press 95.209
Duration: 5:00
Usage: Secular concert
Date: 1987
Level: H.S. - Jr. High

278

Composer: Leavitt, John
Title: Come Follow Me
Voicing: SAB
Accomp: Organ, oboe
Text: Sacred - Come follow me, said Christ the Lord, all in my way abiding...
Range: d4-d5, a3-a4, d3-d4
Difficulty: Med Easy

Style: This is a beautiful and sensitive arrangement of the metrical psalm "Machs mit mir Gott" composed by Bartholomaus Gesius. The oboe solo and accompaniment is an integral part of the composition. The first of the three verses is set for unison voices, the second for two-part women's voices, and the third for a cappella mixed voices. The syncopated rhythm characteristic of metrical psalms makes this an interesting and appealing work. Traditional harmonies.

Comments: Good anthem material for a high school youth choir. Requires a strong oboe soloist.

Publisher: G.I.A. Publications, Inc. G-3028
Usage: Sacred concert - general anthem
Date: 1987
Level: H.S.

279

Composer: Nelson, Ronald A.
Title: Awake, My Soul *
Voicing: SAB

Accomp:	piano
Text:	Sacred - Psalm 106, 108
Range:	c4-a5, Bb3-f5, c2-c4
Difficulty:	Med Easy

Style:	In ABA form with coda. Homophonic. Meter alternates between 6/8 and 2/4 in a lively tempo. Work features frequent open 4ths and 5ths. Mildly dissonant.

Comments:	A relatively easy work for SAB chorus. Rhythmically exciting. A fine work for a young choir.

Publisher:	Augsburg Publishing House 11-0650
Usage:	Sacred - secular concert
Date:	1973
Level:	H.S.

280

Composer:	Papale, Henry
Title:	A Choral Miscellany *
Voicing:	SAB
Accomp:	a cappella
Text:	Secular - Shakespeare, Blake and Tennyson
Range:	e4-b5, b3-e5, ab2-d4 soprano tessitura is a little high
Difficulty:	Med Dif

Style:	This is a set of four pieces utilizing contemporary harmonies and rhythms. The pieces are basically contrapuntal with frequently changing meters and marked dynamic contrasts. The second piece is based on a tone row.

Comments:	A good set for introducing some of the rhythmic complexities and dissonant harmonies of the mid- to late-20th century.

Publisher:	Westwood Press, Inc.
Usage:	Secular concert
Date:	1967
Level:	H.S.

281

Composer:	Pasquet, Jean
Title:	Create in Me a Clean Heart

Voicing:	SAB
Accomp:	Piano
Text:	Sacred - Psalm 51:10-12
Range:	d4-f5, g3-c5, g2-c4
Difficulty:	Med Easy

Style: Homophonic. Flowing with basically quarter-note movement. Fairly traditional harmonies with mild dissonances. Lyrical melodic line.

Comments: A short, but lovely work; quite accessible to the young h.s. chorus.

Publisher:	Augsburg Publishing House 11-0627
Usage:	Sacred - secular concert
Date:	1968
Level:	H.S.

282

Composer:	Roff, Joseph
Title:	To a Mosquito *
Voicing:	SAB
Accomp:	Piano
Text:	Secular - Hail, winged torture, born of ill
Range:	c#4-f#5, Bb3-d5, b2-d4
Difficulty:	MED

Style: The text is humorous and sarcastic. Contrapuntal, unison, and homophonic textures are utilized. The text is set in a mock-classical style. The piano accompaniment is quite important to the overall effect of the piece.

Comments: A fun, lighthearted novelty number. Good for variety on the concert program.

Publisher:	Westwood Press, Inc.
Usage:	Secular concert
Date:	1969
Level:	H.S.

283

Composer:	Schuman, William
Title:	Caution #3 from FOUR ROUNDS ON FAMOUS WORDS
Voicing:	SAB

Accomp:	a cappella
Text:	Secular
Range:	c4-e5, c4-e5, c3-e4
Difficulty:	MED

Style: The work is set in a moderately fast 2/4. It, like the other pieces in this set, is a round. The resulting harmonies are fairly traditional with mild dissonances.

Comments: This is a fun, lighthearted setting which uses as a text three of the old cliches regarding caution: a stitch in time saves nine, etc.

Publisher:	Merion Music Inc.
Usage:	Secular concert
Date:	1957
Level:	H.S.

284

Composer:	Whitecotton, Shirley
Title:	Tubal Cain
Voicing:	SAB
Accomp:	Piano
Text:	Secular - Charles MacKay
Range:	c4-f5, a3-c5, c3-eb4
Difficulty:	Med Easy

Style: Homophonic throughout. Rhythmic movement is principally in quarter and eighth notes at a fairly brisk tempo, but there are no rhythmic difficulties. Tonal with mild dissonance. Wide dynamic range.

Comments: This is scored SA(T)B. The tenor can easily be sung by high school baritones, but it will work well for changing voices also. A relatively simple, straightforward, but exciting work.

Publisher:	Neil A. Kjos, Jr., Publisher EdGC168
Usage:	Secular concert
Date:	1989
Level:	H.S. - Jr. High

285

Composer:	Wood, Dale
Title:	O Praise Ye the Lord

Voicing:	SAB
Accomp:	Organ - optional percussion and brass
Text:	Sacred
Range:	d4-f5(a5), a3-d5, c3-d4
Difficulty:	Med Easy
Style:	A mixture of homophonic and contrapuntal textures. Short exclamatory phrases. Utilizes much unison writing. Mid-section is a three-part canon.
Comments:	Most appropriate as a church anthem but could be used in concert by a h.s. choir.
Publisher:	Harold Flammer Inc. d-5222
Usage:	Sacred - Thanksgiving or general
Date:	1979
Level:	H.S.

286

Composer:	Ahrold, Frank
Title:	Holy Valley
Voicing:	SSA
Accomp:	a cappella
Text:	Secular
Range:	g4-f#5, d4-d5, a3-a4
Difficulty:	Med Easy

Style: A slow, pastoral setting. In a short ABA form the piece is very expressive. Tertian harmonies with some passing tones and added tones adding dissonance. A mixture of homophonic and contrapuntal textures.

Comments: This is a very short piece that would work well with a small SSA ensemble. Good material for a solo and ensemble contest.

Publisher:	Theodore Presser Co. 312-40912
Usage:	Secular concert
Date:	1971
Level:	H.S.

287

Composer:	Baksa, Robert
Title:	Three Precious Gifts
Voicing:	SSA
Accomp:	a cappella
Text:	Secular - Three precious gifts I have today, three precious gifts from heaven.
Range:	e4-f#5, c#4-c#5, a3-a4
Difficulty:	Med Easy

Style: Homophonic with tertian harmonies. This is basically a strophic setting with minor variations between the three verses. In a moderate tempo; rhythmic movement is in quarter and eighth notes.

Comments: This piece would sound well with a young girls' choir. It is not difficult and good for building tone, balance, and blend.

Publisher:	Shawnee Press, Inc. B-423
Duration:	2:35
Usage:	Secular concert

Date: 1976
Level: H.S - Jr. High

                                288

Composer: Baksa, Robert
Title: Songs of Late Summer
Voicing: SSA
Accomp: a cappella
Text: Secular - Texts after ancient Chinese poems
Range: f4-f5, c4-c#5, g3-Bb4
Difficulty: MED

Style: This is a set of three short pieces entitled "Falling Leaves," " Willows,"
                     and "Dawn." Primarily homophonic with some dialogue between paired
                     voices and the third voice. Tertian harmonies with some dissonance,
                     particularly major and minor seconds. The first and last pieces are in a
                     brisk tempo; the second piece is more moderate.

Comments: An attractive set. Pieces may be sung individually or as a group.

Publisher: Shawnee Press, Inc. B-304
Duration: 4:30
Usage: Secular concert
Date: 1969
Level: H.S.

                                289

Composer: Bardos, Lajos
Title: In the Summer *
Voicing: SSA
Accomp: a cappella
Text: Secular-Leaves are budding in the trees
Range: e4-f#5, e4-c#5, g#3-b4
Difficulty: Med Easy

Style: Homophonic; in the spirit of a Hungarian folk song. Triadic throughout.
                     Mild dissonances, lively dotted eighths and triplet figures abound.

Comments: Good material for Spring concert with girls' chorus. Accessible to the
                     average H.S. group.

Publisher: Edward B. Marks MC 4686

SSA

Duration: 1:15
Usage: Secular concert
Date: 1968
Level: H.S.

290

Composer: Bell, Robert Hunter
Title: O Sacrum Convivium
Voicing: SSA
Accomp: a cappella
Text: Sacred
Range: g3-g5, g3-e5, g3-c5
Difficulty: MED

Style: A quiet, sustained setting of this familiar text. Quite dissonant with
                 recurring tone clusters. These clusters are arrived at through diatonic
                 movement in the individual voices. Very interesting contrapuntal
                 writing. The rhythmic movement is entirely in quarter and half notes.

Comments: An excellent introduction to more dissonant twentieth-century music.
                 The tone clusters are approached through stepwise movement so that
                 the dissonances are not problematic for the singers. A good teaching
                 tool, but also effective program material.

Publisher: Gordon V. Thompson G-324
Usage: Sacred Concert
Date: 1985
Level: H.S.

291

Composer: Britten, Benjamin
Title: Country Girls from CHORAL DANCES FROM GLORIANA
Voicing: SA
Accomp: a cappella
Text: Secular - Sweet flag and cuckooflower, cowslip and columbine...
Range: a4-a5, d4-d5
Difficulty: MED

Style: The piece is in a question and answer style; soprano voice characterized
                 by a dotted eighth-note figure answered by a slightly syncopated
                 response in the alto. The mild dissonances are really coincidental, a
                 result of the simultaneous singing of the two parts.

Comments: A fun and singable work for girls' chorus. The independence of the two voice parts should make learning this piece relatively easy.

Publisher: Boosey & Hawkes   (Set 17411)
Usage: Secular concert
Date: 1954
Level: H.S. - college

292

Composer: Butler, Eugene
Title: Hunting Song
Voicing: SSA
Accomp: Piano
Text: Secular - Sir Walter Scott
Range: e4-e5, e4-d5, e4-b4
Difficulty: Med Easy

Style: An exciting piece for girls' chorus. The use of open fifths in the accompaniment and rapidly moving eighth notes in both the vocal and accompaniment lines lend a gypsy quality to the music. The vocal writing is principally a two-voice texture with three voices used at cadences and at points of exclamation. Rhythmic but not difficult. Tertian harmonies with mild dissonances.

Comments: A good work for developing clean diction and rhythmic precision in the girls' chorus. An exciting piece.

Publisher: Paul A. Schmitt Music Co. SCHCH02590
Usage: Secular concert
Date: 1975
Level: H.S. - Junior High

293

Composer: Casals, Pablo
Title: Nigra Sum
Voicing: SSA
Accomp: Piano
Text: Sacred - I am black, but comely, o ye daughters of Jerusalem.
Range: b3-g5, b3-f#5, a3-e5
Difficulty: Med Easy

Style:	The rich sonorities created in the accompaniment make this an exciting work. The vocal lines are relatively simple. Tertian harmonies. The first half of the octavo is set for two part chorus, and the final half alternates between three-voice and unison textures. Homophonic and only mildly dissonant. Calls for sustained singing and careful attention to line and phrasing.
Comments:	A relatively simple and easy, but beautiful work. Good for developing phrasing in the girls' chorus.
Publisher:	Tetra Music Corp. TC120
Duration:	5:00
Usage:	Sacred - secular concert
Date:	1966
Level:	H.S. - College

294

Composer:	Casals, Pablo
Title:	Canco a la Verge (Hymn to the Virgin)
Voicing:	SA
Accomp:	Organ or Piano
Text:	Sacred
Range:	a3-f5, a3-f5
Difficulty:	Easy
Style:	This anthem opens with a unison chorus, then moves into a two-part strophic setting of the three verses of the text. Homophonic with tertian harmonies. Primary rhythmic movement is in eighth notes at a moderate tempo. The rich romantic character of Casals' music is apparent in the bass line of the accompaniment.
Comments:	A very simple but beautiful work.
Publisher:	Tetra Music Corp. A.B. 138-4
Usage:	Sacred-secular concert
Date:	1968
Level:	H.S.

295

Composer:	Crocker, Emily
Title:	Two Songs of Longing
Voicing:	SSA

Accomp:	a cappella
Text:	Secular - John Donne and Matthew Arnold
Range:	d4-g5, d4-d5, a3-d5
Difficulty:	Med Easy

Style: Both of these short pieces utilize a mixture of contrapuntal and homophonic textures. There is a limited use of paired voices set against the third voice and some use of short imitative figures. Tertian harmonies. The movement in the voice parts is basically conjunct. Both texts are set sensitively, and the tempo is moderate.

Comments: Good program material. Both of these pieces sound well with high school voices. The works would be useful in developing a well balanced and blended tone.

Publisher:	Jenson Publications, Inc.
Usage:	Secular concert
Date:	1985
Level:	H.S.

296

Composer:	Distler, Hugo
Title:	Lift Up Your Heads, Ye Mighty Gates
Voicing:	SSA
Accomp:	a cappella
Text:	Sacred - hymn text
Range:	g4-e5, d4-b5, g3-g4
Difficulty:	MED

Style: Contrapuntal with the chant-like vocal independence characteristic of Distler's music. Rhythmic displacement results from the contrapuntal texture. Chorale tune appears in 1st soprano while other voices move freely. Frequently changing meters.

Comments: A challenging work for the average h.s. chorus. Helpful in developing vocal independence.

Publisher:	Arista Music, Inc. AE128
Usage:	Secular - sacred concert
Date:	1967
Level:	H.S.

297

Composer:	Distler, Hugo
Title:	Lied vom Winde
Voicing:	SSA
Accomp:	a cappella
Text:	Secular - German and English - Song of the Winds
Range:	a3-e5, b3-e5
Difficulty:	MED

Style: Alternates between a moderate 3/4 and a 3/8 that is to be sung as fast as possible. Rhythmic and quite repetitive. The piece gradually slows to the end. Extensive use of 3rds and 5ths. Fairly traditional harmonies.

Comments: An interesting and lively chorus for treble voices.

Publisher:	Joseph Boonin, Inc. B 241
Usage:	Secular concert
Date:	1975
Level:	H.S.

298

Composer:	Donato, Anthony
Title:	Song for Evening
Voicing:	SSA
Accomp:	a cappella
Text:	Secular - Jeanne DeLamarter
Range:	c4-a5, Bb3-Eb5, f3-c5
Difficulty:	MED

Style: The composer uses a mixture of homophonic and contrapuntal textures in this piece. The harmony is primarily tertian with mild dissonances. Rhythmic movement is principally in eighth and quarter notes and is not problematic.

Comments: This would be an effective piece for most any high school girls' chorus although the alto tessitura is a little low for most high school altos. This is an accessible and charming work.

Publisher:	Peer-Southern 93-5
Usage:	Secular concert
Date:	1951
Level:	H.S.

299

Composer:	Durufle, Maurice
Title:	Tota Pulchra from QUATRE MOTETS
Voicing:	SSA
Accomp:	a cappella
Text:	Sacred - Tota pulchra es, Maria, et Macula originalis non est in te...
Range:	d4-a5, a3-d5, g3-c5
Difficulty:	Med Dif

Style: The rhythm of the original Gregorian chant dictates a frequently changing meter throughout the motet. The texture is primarily contrapuntal, and the harmonies are traditional with dissonances resulting from passing tones and occasional added tones.

Comments: An extraordinarily beautiful motet, but it requires a mature girls' chorus for successful performance. The tessitura of the alto line is very low. There is some divisi writing in both the second soprano and alto lines.

Publisher:	Durand S.A.
Usage:	Sacred - secular concert
Date:	1960
Level:	H.S. - College

300

Composer:	Duson, Dede
Title:	In Unison
Voicing:	SSAA
Accomp:	Violin and Clarinet
Text:	Secular - Gwen Frostic
Range:	Bb3-g5, a3-eb5
Difficulty:	MED

Style: The piece is scored primarily for two voices with some divisi writing at cadences. Changing meters throughout. Homophonic and mildly dissonant. The violin and clarinet accompaniment nicely complements the vocal lines. 5/8 meter is used extensively, and it, combined with the changing meters, adds rhythmic interest to the work.

Comments: Well written for h.s. girls' chorus. The text is particularly appropriate for h.s. singers as well.

Publisher:	Neil A. Kjos Music Co. Ed. 6200
Usage:	Secular concert
Date:	1988
Level:	H.S.

301

Composer:	Duson, Dede
Title:	And Back Again
Voicing:	SSAA
Accomp:	a cappella
Text:	Secular - In rhythmic rotation the earth travels ever around the sun
Range:	c4-a5, g3-e5
Difficulty:	MED

Style: Lilting movement in 6/8 in outer sections; central section is slower and more homophonic. Mixture of contrapuntal and homophonic textures; much use of simultaneous, paired duets. Fairly traditional harmonies; mildly dissonant.

Comments: A beautiful work for women's voices. Excellent material. Written for the South Houston H.S. Girls' Choir's performance at the 1981 ACDA national convention.

Publisher:	Jenson Publications 413-01033
Usage:	Secular concert
Date:	1981
Level:	H.S.

302

Composer:	Felciano, Richard
Title:	Cosmic Festival from TWO PUBLIC PIECES
Voicing:	Unison
Accomp:	Electronic tape
Text:	Secular - Elizabeth Barrett Browning
Range:	c4-d5
Difficulty:	Easy

Style: The work features electronic tape and 4 melodic patterns that are to be sung in the sequence indicated by the composer. Achieves a cyclic effect. The melodic patterns are in 3/8 and are sung lightly and effortlessly.

Comments: The composer indicates ways to utilize audience participation, children's voices, and slide projections. A simple but novel work.

Publisher: E. C. Schirmer Music Co. 2938
Duration: 6:34
Usage: Sacred - secular concert
Date: 1972
Level: H.S.

303

Composer: Felciano, Richard
Title: The Not-Yet Flower (A Crisis of Growth) from TWO PUBLIC PIECES
Voicing: Unison
Accomp: Electronic tape
Text: Secular
Range: c4-e5
Difficulty: Easy

Style: This piece is similar to the 1st piece in the set in that it features unison voices with tape accompaniment. The singing is soft and non-assertive. Readings from current articles (news items) are to be read by audience participants. Short melodic patterns are utilized.

Comments: A simple piece, interesting mainly for its novel effects.

Publisher: E.C. Schirmer Music Co.
Usage: Secular concert
Date: 1972
Level: H.S.

304

Composer: Felciano, Richard
Title: O Come, O Come Emmanuel
Voicing: SSA
Accomp: a cappella
Text: Sacred - traditional chant
Range: f4-f5, Bb3-eb5, g3-eb5
Difficulty: Easy

Style: An arrangement of the traditional tune. Melody is first stated in unison, but the refrain is set homophonically. Second verse is set contrapuntally with homophonic refrain. Traditional harmonies are accented with passing tones and suspensions that lend a contemporary flavor to the familiar work.

Comments: Quite accessible for the girls' chorus. Good program material for the developing choir.

Publisher: Edward B. Marks MC4319
Usage: Christmas
Date: 1965
Level: H.S.

305

Composer: Forsyth, Malcolm
Title: Three Zulu Songs
Voicing: SSA
Accomp: Flute, oboe, hand drum
Text: Zulu songs by V.W. Vilakazi (South Africa) Hail Wind, The Moon, The Valley of a Thousand Hills
Range: f4-a5, d4-f5, a3-c5
Difficulty: MED

Style: All three of these pieces are highly rhythmic; the first is in a faster tempo [quarter note=120] while the second two are slower. Each piece utilizes handclapping, finger snapping and tongue clicks. Melodically and harmonically the pieces are readily accessible; some quartal harmonies. Melodies tend to be repetitive and restricted in range. The Zulu pronunciation will require practice, but a guide is provided. Interesting pieces.

Comments: These are particularly timely pieces with the current interest in South Africa. They would provide an exciting and interesting introduction to ethnic music in a contemporary setting.

Publisher: Gordon V. Thompson Music G-333
Usage: Secular Concert
Date: 1989
Level: Children - H.S.

306

Composer: Frackenpohl, Arthur
Title: Hogamus, Higamus *

Voicing: Speaking chorus (Three-voice)
Accomp: Percussion instruments
Text: Secular - Hogamus, higamus, men are polygamous
Range:
Difficulty: Med Dif

Style: A double fugue for speaking chorus and percussion. Some vocal inflection is neccessary for effective performance. Lively tempo.

Comments: An interesting rhythmic exercise. Would give variety to typical choral program.

Publisher: Piedmont Music Co. (Edward B. Marks)
Duration: 2:45
Usage: Secular concert
Date: 1966
Level: H.S.

307

Composer: Harper, John
Title: Psalm 150
Voicing: SA/TB
Accomp: Organ
Text: Sacred - Psalm 150 - Praise God in his holy place, praise him in his mighty heavens...
Range: a4-e5, d4-e5
Difficulty: Easy

Style: The melodic writing is angular and restricted in range. Minor dissonances occur through passing and added tones. Most of the writing is unison with two parts used to accentuate text painting at the words "praise him with resounding cymbals. The organ accompaniment complements the vocal writing. The piece is rhythmic throughout.

Comments: This work would be an effective introit for a high school or adult choir. A short but powerful piece.

Publisher: Oxford University Press E135
Usage: Sacred concert - General anthem
Date: 1974
Level: H.S. - Junior High

308

Composer:	Harris, Robert A.
Title:	The Lamb
Voicing:	SSAA
Accomp:	a cappella
Text:	Sacred - William Blake
Range:	d4-a5, c4-e5, g3-d5, f#3-d5
Difficulty:	Med Dif

Style: The texture of this piece is contrapuntal throughout; the voice parts are written so that there is a constantly shifting dialogue among the individual voices. The harmonies are tonal and traditional but colored by frequent added tones. Although the tempo is moderate, rhythmic interest occurs through syncopation and dotted quarter/eighth-note figures. The composer has given careful attention to text underlay.

Comments: This is a fresh setting of Blake's familiar text. The alto lines are quite low, but otherwise this is excellent material for a high school girls' chorus. Outstanding concert material.

Publisher:	Oxford University Press 94.407
Duration:	1:00
Usage:	Sacred - Secular concert
Date:	1988
Level:	H.S.

309

Composer:	Henderson, Ruth Watson
Title:	The Yak and The Train Dogs (Musical Animal Tales Set II)
Voicing:	SA
Accomp:	Piano
Text:	Secular - Children's animal tales
Range:	e4-g5, c4-e5
Difficulty:	Easy

Style: These two pieces alternate between unison and two-part writing. Frequent major and minor seconds in the harmonic structure, but these dissonances are generally approached by step. The rhythmic movement in the accompaniment complements the vocal writing. The voice parts are principally conjunct.

Comments: These pieces are two short musical animal tales written for the Toronto
              Children's Choir, but will work well with either a junior high or young
              high school girls' chorus.

Publisher: Gordon V. Thompson Music G-222
Usage: Secular concert
Date: 1981
Level: Children - H.S.

                                        310

Composer: Henderson, Ruth Watson
Title: Storm from THROUGH THE EYES OF CHILDREN
Voicing: SA
Accomp: Piano and Orff instruments
Text: Secular - Poetry written by Canadian primary school children - The dark
              sky hangs heavily...
Range: e4-f5
Difficulty: Med Easy

Style: Written for two groups of singers: choir A carries the melody and text
              in unison, while the B choir part is in speech-song. The
              accompaniment is dissonant to be descriptive of the text. The melodic
              line is conjunct and singable. The B choir part is entirely speech-song
              and presents a rhythmic accompaniment to the vocal line of choir A.

Comments: This was written as a children's piece but would work well with junior
              high or even high school singers. A delightful work. A good
              introduction to 20th-century techniques, particularly speech-song.

Publisher: Gordon V. Thompson G-230
Usage: Secular concert
Date: 1984
Level: Children - H.S.

                                        311

Composer: Hennagin, Michael
Title: Three Emily Dickinson Songs
Voicing: SA
Accomp: Piano
Text: Secular-1)Heart, We Will Forget Him 2)Going to Heaven 3)The World
              Feels Dusty
Range: a3-a5, g3-eb5

Difficulty:	Diff
Style:	The first and last songs are set in a slow tempo in contrast to the much longer and rapidly moving second song. All three are quite dissonant with disjunct melodic lines. Interesting but complex accompaniment. The second song is episodic with a recurring refrain. Changing meters.
Comments:	This is challenging literature, but would be excellent material for an advanced girls' choir. Beautifully sensitive settings of the texts. An extended work.
Publisher:	Walton Music Corp. M-139
Usage:	Secular concert
Date:	1976
Level:	H.S. - college

312

Composer:	Holland, Wilfrid
Title:	A New Year Carol
Voicing:	SA
Accomp:	Piano
Text:	Sacred - Here we bring new water from the well so clear, for to worship God, this Happy New Year.
Range:	f4-g5, d4-f5
Difficulty:	Easy
Style:	Traditional tertian harmonies. In a joyous 6/8 meter, this New Year's Day song is a delightful setting of a traditional text from South Wales. Both parts are quite melodic making for interesting contrapuntal writing. A simple piano accompaniment complements the vocal writing.
Comments:	Suitable for a children's choir or a young high school girls' chorus. Very singable. Good material for a mid-winter concert.
Publisher:	E.C. Schirmer
Usage:	New Year's Day Anthem -Sacred concert
Date:	1987
Level:	H.S. - children

313

Composer:	Holland, Wilfrid
Title:	A Rustic Song
Voicing:	SSA
Accomp:	Piano
Text:	Secular - What a dainty life the milkmaid leads
Range:	f#4-g5, e4-g5, a3-b4
Difficulty:	MED

Style: This short piece is in a lilting 9/8 meter [dotted quarter=50]. Rhythmically, the voice parts are characterized by dotted eighth/sixteenth-note figures and sixteenth-note groupings. Tertian harmonies. The texture is a mixture of homophonic and contrapuntal styles.

Comments: A charming piece for the girls' chorus. The second soprano line has one high g, but otherwise lies well within the second soprano range.

Publisher:	E.C. Schirmer 2842
Usage:	Secular concert
Date:	1983
Level:	H.S.

314

Composer:	Holst, Gustav T.
Title:	Hymn to Vena from CHORAL HYMNS FROM THE RIG VEDA (Group 3, no. 3)
Voicing:	SSAA
Accomp:	Harp or piano
Text:	Secular - The sun rising through the mist.
Range:	d4-ab5, d4-g5, b3-d5, g3-c5
Difficulty:	Diff

Style: The vocal parts are set homophonically over a dramatic and rapidly changing accompaniment. Tertian harmonies but with liberal use of chromatics and frequent seventh chords. The rhythm in the voice parts is straightforward, but the tempo changes frequently.

Comments: This is a dramatic work, best suited for a festival or large chorus. An exciting but demanding work.

Publisher:	Belwin Mills Publishing Corp. GMOD 289
Usage:	Festival - secular concert

Date: 1912
Level: H.S. - College

315

Composer: Hovhaness, Alan
Title: O Lady Moon *
Voicing: SSA
Accomp: Clarinet and piano
Text: Secular poem by Lafcadio Hearn - O Lady Moon, I saw a cat and a rat
                         carrying a barrel of sake.
Range: d4-g5, d4-e5, g3-c4
Difficulty: Med Dif

Style: Mixture of homophonic and contrapuntal textures. Long eighth-note
                         melismas in all voices. Tonal, in g minor. Flowing with quarter note
                         pulse=80. Dialogue between clarinet and voices.

Comments: Requires a good 1st soprano section and fairly confident girls' chorus.
                         Clarinet accompaniment adds interesting timbre to the work.

Publisher: Edward B. Marks MC4653
Usage: Secular concert
Date: 1976
Level: H.S.

316

Composer: Hovland, Egil
Title: Laudate Dominum
Voicing: SSA
Accomp: a cappella
Text: Sacred - Psalm 150 - Latin (English)
Range: c4-a5, c4-f#5, a3-d5
Difficulty: Med Dif

Style: Extensive canonic writing alternating with sections in which two paired
                         voices are set against the independent 3rd voice. Moves in and out of
                         cluster patterns. Basically conjunct movement in voices. Parts are
                         singable although total effect is quite dissonant.

Comments: An interesting work for an advanced girls' chorus. Driving, repetitive
                         rhythms and syncopation.

Publisher:	Walton Music Corp
Usage:	Secular - sacred concert
Date:	1980
Level:	H.S.

317

Composer:	Kodaly, Zoltan
Title:	Dancing Song
Voicing:	SSA
Accomp:	a cappella
Text:	Secular - Traditional Hungarian folksong. People say the Magyars now no more are lightfooted.
Range:	d4-f5(a5), g3-c5
Difficulty:	Med Easy
Style:	Fast folk dance. Imitative, canonic treatment throughout. Constantly changing contrapuntal texture. Tempo builds to a final "presto."
Comments:	Excellent piece for developing vocal independence. Not a beginners' work. Medium level girls' chorus.

Publisher:	Oxford University Press 54.942
Usage:	Secular concert
Date:	1933
Level:	H.S.

318

Composer:	Kodaly, Zoltan
Title:	The Straw Guy
Voicing:	SSAA
Accomp:	a cappella
Text:	Secular - Hungarian folksong - Tell us, pray, who owns this house? Johnny Martin owns this house, Straw Guy.
Range:	d4-eb5, g3-ab4
Difficulty:	Easy
Style:	Hungarian folk dance. Homophonic; through-composed. Triadic. Lively tempo with eighth- and quarter-note movement.
Comments:	A lively folk setting accessible to most h.s. girls' choruses. May be used to help build vocal independence in part singing while providing interesting program material.

Publisher:	Oxford University Press 54.916
Usage:	Secular concert
Date:	1925
Level:	H.S.

319

Composer:	Kodaly, Zoltan
Title:	St. Gregory's Day
Voicing:	SSA
Accomp:	a cappella
Text:	Secular - Hungarian folk song
Range:	d4-f#5, g3-a4
Difficulty:	Easy

Style:	Hungarian folksong. Lively dance tune in fast eighth- and quarter-note movement. Triadic. Sectional piece opening with homophonic texture, then moving into contrapuntal figures accompanying the melodic line.
Comments:	Easily accessible for young high school girls' chorus. Good teaching piece for part singing. Interesting program material.
Publisher:	Oxford University Press W.39
Usage:	Secular concert
Date:	1933
Level:	H.S.

320

Composer:	Krenek, Ernst
Title:	In Paradisum
Voicing:	SSA
Accomp:	a cappella
Text:	Latin - text from the Requiem Mass
Range:	g4-g5, d4-e5, a3-c5
Difficulty:	MED

Style:	Contrapuntal. Tertian harmonies, with some sharp dissonances, particularly major and minor seconds. In triple meter the piece moves quietly but with some animation [quarter note=120]. For most of the piece the first soprano line floats well above the other two voices. Effective use of suspension figures.
Comments:	A lovely work for girls' chorus.

Publisher: Rongwen Music, Inc.
Usage: Sacred - secular concert
Date: 1966
Level: H.S.

321

Composer: Lekberg, Sven
Title: Let All the World in Every Corner Sing
Voicing: SSA (SSAA)
Accomp: a cappella
Text: Sacred - Let all the world in every corner sing, my God and King
Range: g4-a5, eb4-f5, c4-db5
Difficulty: Med Dif

Style: Primarily homophonic. A festive piece with vigorous rhythmic movement. Much use of added tones and alternation between major and minor modes. Recurrent refrain throughout the work.

Comments: Good piece for girls' choir that can handle four-part divisi. Best for above average girls' group.

Publisher: G. Schirmer 11843
Usage: Sacred-secular concert
Date: 1969
Level: H.S.

322

Composer: MacGillivray, Allister
Title: Song for the Mira
Voicing: SSA
Accomp: Piano and oboe
Text: Secular - the Mira is a river in Cape Breton (Canada)
Range: d4-f#5, d4-d5, g#3-d5
Difficulty: Med Easy

Style: This is actually an arrangement by Stuart Calvert and therefore falls outside of the general critera used for most entries in this work; however, the careful and skillful arrangement merits performance by high school groups. It opens with an accompanied oboe solo, followed by a solo statement of the first two verses of the text. The remainder of the work is in the form of a theme and variations with each new verse and refrain treated in a distinctive style.   Tuneful melody and consonant harmonies.

Comments: An excellent piece for a girls' chorus. The beautiful melodic line, the oboe accompaniment, and the simple variations will make this a favorite for singers and audience alike.

Publisher: Gordon V. Thompson Music G-326
Usage: Secular concert
Date: 1986
Level: H.S.

323

Composer: Marshall, Jane
Title: Lift Up Your Heads
Voicing: SSA
Accomp: Piano, handbells
Text: Sacred - Psalm 24
Range: c#4-f5, c#4-f5, c#4-f5
Difficulty: Easy

Style: This is actually a unison anthem that includes three short optional divisi statements. The vocal line is melodic and primarily conjunct. The accompaniment is arpeggiated in the right hand over chordal half-note movement in the left hand. The formal structure is ABA with a short coda.

Comments: An excellent piece for a church youth choir or a high school girls' chorus. The piece was written for a children's choir festival but works well with unison high school girls. Good for developing range, blend, and balance.

Publisher: Hinshaw Music, Inc. HMC-972
Usage: Sacred concert - Palm Sunday, General
Date: 1988
Level: H.S.

324

Composer: McElheran, Brock
Title: Here Comes the Avant-Garde
Voicing: Mixed - Men or Women
Accomp: Piano & Percussion with optional electronic tape

Text: Secular - narration illustrated by nonsense syllables
Range:
Difficulty: Med Easy

Style: A tour de force of avant garde techniques. Narrator explains and chorus demonstrates.

Comments: A novelty piece that would serve as a good introduction to avant garde music for both the audience and the chorus.

Publisher: Oxford University Press
Usage: Secular concert
Date: 1969
Level: H.S.

325

Composer: McElheran, Brock
Title: Funeral March on the Deaths of Heroes
Voicing: Mixed - Men or Women - Speaking chorus
Accomp: a cappella
Text: Names of fallen soldiers
Range:
Difficulty: Easy

Style: Avant garde. Repetition of different names simultaneously; builds in intensity then recedes, ending in a unison coda.

Comments: Good introduction to avant garde speech techniques. Would be most effective with a medium to large chorus.

Publisher: Oxford University Press
Usage: Secular concert
Date: 1969
Level: H.S.

326

Composer: Mechem, Kirke
Title: A Farewell
Voicing: SA Unison
Accomp: Piano
Text: Secular - Harriet Monroe - Goodbye! No, do not grieve that it is over, the perfect hour.

Range:	c#4-d5
Difficulty:	Med Easy

Style: The unison vocal line is a simple, diatonic, melodic line which floats lightly over an interesting accompaniment. The right hand of the accompaniment is in two voices in continuous movement over an ostinato figure in the bass line.

Comments: A beautiful and effective unison work. This would be a lovely piece for any girls' chorus, but would be sung with greater feeling and understanding by a more mature high school ensemble.

Publisher:	E.C. Schirmer 2825
Usage:	Secular concert
Date:	1968
Level:	H.S.

327

Composer:	Mechem, Kirke
Title:	The Cynic
Voicing:	SA
Accomp:	Piano
Text:	Secular - Theodosia Garrison
Range:	Bb3-g5, a3-eb5
Difficulty:	Med Diff

Style: In a brisk tempo (quarter note = 150); Mechem has set the voices in metrical opposition with 6/8 against 3/4 throughout. The work is canonic, but each repetition of the canon is varied by pitch, inversion or rhythm. A great deal of chromaticism; quite dissonant.

Comments: A difficult two-part piece. Not a beginning work; however, if the individual lines are learned melodically and independently, this would make an exciting and fun work for a good girls' chorus.

Publisher:	E.C. Schirmer 2824
Usage:	Secular concert
Date:	1968
Level:	H.S.

328

Composer:	Mechem, Kirke
Title:	The Message #2 from THE WINGED JOY
Voicing:	SSA
Accomp:	Piano
Text:	Secular
Range:	Bb3-g5, ab3-d5
Difficulty:	MED

Style: This is the second piece in a group of seven written as a seven-part love story. Lively and rhythmic employing a very fast tempo. Occasional changing meters. Basically contrapuntal. Mild dissonances.

Comments: A lively, expressive work with an attractive accompaniment. Soprano solo.

Publisher:	E.C. Schirmer
Usage:	Secular concert
Date:	1968
Level:	H.S.

329

Composer:	Mellnas, Arne
Title:	Aglepta
Voicing:	SSA
Accomp:	a cappella
Text:	Secular - Swedish troll proverb - To leave an enemy without my answer...
Range:	ab4-f#5, f4-Bb4, a3-a4
Difficulty:	Med Easy

Style: Avant garde. Whispering, glissandi, tone clusters, speech, etc. Utilizes new notational systems. Pitches are all related to other parts and are easily singable.

Comments: A good introduction to avant garde sounds and notation. Easily accessible to H.S. chorus.

Publisher:	Walton Music Corp
Usage:	Secular concert
Date:	1969
Level:	H.S.

330

Composer:	Nelhybel, Vaclav
Title:	When Love is Kind
Voicing:	SSA
Accomp:	Piano
Text:	Secular - When love is kind, cheerful and free.
Range:	c4-g5, c4-d5, a3-d5
Difficulty:	MED

Style: An interesting and novel arrangement of this traditional English air. The piano accompaniment is rhythmic and utilizes frequent syncopation. The harmony is traditional but includes a number of passing tones adding some light dissonance to the work.

Comments: A delightful setting of this familiar tune. Good material for any high school girls' chorus. Very singable.

Publisher:	J. Christopher Music Co. JCMC14
Usage:	Secular concert
Date:	1981
Level:	H.S.

331

Composer:	Page, Robert
Title:	Quem vidistis pastores from THREE CHRISTMAS MOTETS
Voicing:	SSA - SATB - TBB
Accomp:	a cappella
Text:	Sacred
Range:	a3-g#5, g#3-c#5, eb3-a4, e2-f4 Fairly extreme ranges in sop & bass
Difficulty:	Diff

Style: Frequent tempo and meter changes. Quite dissonant. Alternation between legato passages and more rhythmic marcato sections. Both homophonic and contrapuntal textures are employed. Three ensembles are needed for performance. These SSA, SATB, and TTB sections alternate throughout the work with occasional simultaneous sounding of all three ensembles.

Comments: An interesting work but requires a strong choral ensemble for a successful performance. Only a large and quite advanced h.s. choir should attempt this piece.

Publisher: Standard Music Publishing, Inc.
Usage: Sacred concert - Christmas and/or festival
Date: 1971
Level: H.S. - college

332

Composer: Persichetti, Vincent
Title: Nouns to Nouns
Voicing: SA/TB
Accomp: Piano
Text: Secular - e.e. cummings
Range: e4-f5, b3-b4
Difficulty: MED

Style: In a lively tempo this piece is rhythmic with frequent use of
               syncopation. The texture alternates between homophonic and
               contrapuntal styles. Mildly dissonant vocal parts with greater dissonance
               in the accompaniment.

Comments: A delightful setting of this e.e. cummings text. Good material for either
               two-part girls' or boys' chorus.

Publisher: Elkan-Vogel, Inc. 362-01223
Usage: Secular concert
Date: 1966
Level: H.S.

333

Composer: Pierce, Brent
Title: My Love Has Gone
Voicing: SA / TB
Accomp: Piano
Text: Secular
Range: d4-e5, g3-Bb4
Difficulty: Easy

Style: Contrapuntal throughout. Pierce uses some interesting text painting
               through his rhythms and dynamics. Although the rhythmic construction
               in the work is not complex, it intensifies to heighten climactic sections.

Mildly dissonant. The accompaniment imitates ringing bells throughout the work.

Comments: This work is best suited for girls' voices. The range of the alto line is too low for tenors and young basses. This is an interesting piece for girls' chorus and would be useful in developing light, sensitive singing.

Publisher: Plymouth Music Co., Inc. BP - 505
Usage: Secular concert
Date: 1981
Level: H.S.

334

Composer: Pierce, Brent
Title: Dance of the One-Legged Sailor
Voicing: SA / TB
Accomp: Piano
Text: Secular
Range: c4-g5, g3-b4
Difficulty: Med Easy

Style: As the title might indicate, the piece is set in mixed meter, alternating between 6/8, 3/4 and 5/8 time. The tempo is brisk with the dotted quarter=104. The texture is a mixture of homophonic and contrapuntal styles. There is generous use of open fifths and parallel octaves in the accompaniment. Mildly dissonant, mostly in the accompaniment part.

Comments: A rhythmically interesting and fun piece. Good material for a boys' chorus.

Publisher: Plymouth Music Co., Inc. BP.502
Usage: Secular concert
Date: 1981
Level: H.S.

335

Composer: Pierce, Brent
Title: Gloria in Excelsis Deo
Voicing: SA / TB
Accomp: Piano
Text: Sacred
Range: c4-f5, c4-e5

Difficulty: Med Easy

Style: The texture of this piece is primarily contrapuntal punctuated by short homophonic statements. Mildly dissonant. In 6/8 time the work is rhythmically interesting but presents no particular difficulties. Melodic movement is principally conjunct.

Comments: An interesting two-part work, well suited to either an intermediate level girls' or boys' chorus.

Publisher: Plymouth Music Co., Inc. BP.503
Usage: Sacred - secular concert
Date: 1981
Level: H.S.

336

Composer: Pierce, Brent
Title: Come and Follow Me
Voicing: SA / TB
Accomp: Piano
Text: Secular - Come and follow me across the sea. Come and be my love...
Range: g3-d5, g3-d5
Difficulty: Easy

Style: With the exception of a six-bar phrase, this piece is written entirely as a two-part canon. The vocal lines are conjunct. The accompaniment is somewhat dissonant. Basic rhythmic movement is by eighth notes in duple meter.

Comments: This would be good material for a young chorus. Although the piece is indicated for SA or TB, the voicing works best for girls.

Publisher: Plymouth Music Co., Inc. BP.501
Usage: Secular concert
Date: 1981
Level: H.S. - Junior High

337

Composer: Pinkham, Daniel
Title: Memory, hither come
Voicing: SA
Accomp: a cappella

Text:	Secular - William Blake
Range:	d4-g5, b3-d5
Difficulty:	MED

Style: In ABA form, the B section is in a slow duple meter contrasting with the faster, dance-like outer sections that alternate between 9/8 and 12/8 time. The outer sections are somewhat chromatic with frequent dissonances. The sustained B section utilizes tertian harmonies with numerous suspension figures.

Comments: This is a well crafted work. Useful as an introduction to slightly more dissonant twentieth-century techniques. Good material for an intermediate to advanced girls' chorus.

Publisher:	E.C. Schirmer 2819
Usage:	Secular concert
Date:	1979
Level:	H.S.

338

Composer:	Rutter, John
Title:	The Heavenly Aeroplane
Voicing:	SA
Accomp:	Piano, double bass, drums
Text:	Secular - based on an Ozark folksong (c. 1935)
Range:	c4-ab5, c4-f5
Difficulty:	Med Easy

Style: In an early rock-and-roll style, the piece is highly syncopated. The melody is primarily diatonic with frequent chromatic movement; the two-part harmony is principally in sixths. Piano accompaniment is in a rock-and-roll, gospel style.

Comments: Although this piece is an exception in style to the majority of selections in this bibliography, it is included because of its unique and engaging treatment of a "religious" text. A must for high school girls' chorus.

Publisher:	Oxford University Press T114
Usage:	Sacred-secular concert
Date:	1985
Level:	H.S.

339

Composer:	Rutter, John
Title:	For the Beauty of the Earth
Voicing:	SA or two-part choir
Accomp:	Piano
Text:	Sacred - For the beauty of the earth, for the beauty of the skies
Range:	d4-g5, a3-e5,
Difficulty:	Easy

Style: A lyrical melodic line over an arpeggiated accompaniment figure in piano. Has the feel of a popular song; rather light and easy.

Comments: An accessible, singable piece for either young mixed chorus or girls' chorus.

Publisher:	Hinshaw Music Inc. HMC-469
Usage:	Sacred - secular concert
Date:	1980
Level:	H.S.

340

Composer:	Sateren, Leland B.
Title:	Outdoor Three
Voicing:	SSA
Accomp:	Piano
Text:	Secular - Thomas Wensell - 1)Lone Fisherman; 2)Cross Country; 3)The Firefly
Range:	a3-a5, a3-f5, a3-f5
Difficulty:	Med Easy

Style: The texture is homophonic. The first of this set of three pieces moves slowly in quarter notes, the second more rapidly in quarter- and eighth-note patterns. The third piece is for unison voices.

Comments: This set was commissioned for a boys' chorus, but it would work well with a girls' choir. A lovely set.

Publisher:	Curtis Music Press C8517
Usage:	Secular concert
Date:	1985
Level:	H.S.

341

Composer:	Smith, Russell
Title:	We Talked as Girls Do from THREE SONGS FROM EMILY DICKINSON *
Voicing:	SSA
Accomp:	a cappella
Text:	Secular poem by Emily Dickinson
Range:	e4-g5, c#4-e5, a3-a4
Difficulty:	Med Dif

Style: Mixture of homophonic and contrapuntal textures. Long phrases. Tonal but includes close dissonances. Voice leading is mostly conjunct with flowing lines.

Comments: A beautiful piece for girls' chorus or for small SSA ensemble.

Publisher:	Franco Columbo Inc.
Usage:	Secular concert
Date:	1963
Level:	H.S.

342

Composer:	Stravinsky, Igor
Title:	Four Russian Peasant Songs *
Voicing:	SSAA or TTBB solos in each voice part
Accomp:	a cappella
Text:	Secular English and Russian texts
Range:	e4-f5, e4-e5, b3-d4, a3-a4
Difficulty:	Med Dif

Style: Frequently changing meters and varied rhythmic effects. Extensive unison and two-part writing. Melodic lines lie within restricted ranges. Work is typical of early Stravinsky; close harmony, frequent 2nds, highly rhythmic and somewhat repetitive.

Comments: Good introduction to Stravinsky. Set may be performed in its entirety or individual pieces may be performed separately.

Publisher:	Edward B. Marks Music Corp. MC27
Duration:	4:
Usage:	Secular concert
Date:	1917
Level:	H.S.

343

Composer:	Tate, Phyllis
Title:	The Frog in the Well
Voicing:	SSA
Accomp:	a cappella
Text:	Secular - There was a frog lived in the spring, sing song kitty can't you kimey-o.
Range:	Bb3-g5, g3-eb5
Difficulty:	Med Easy

Style: Homophonic; tonal. Clever setting of an old folk tune. Theme and variations: harmonic, rhythmic, and melodic variations are used. Lively tempo, half note=96. Quarter- and eighth-note movement.

Comments: Requires wide range in 2nd sopranos and altos. A fun and novel setting of this old favorite.

Publisher:	Oxford University Press
Usage:	Secular concert
Date:	1955
Level:	H.S.

344

Composer:	Thompson, Randall
Title:	Solstice
Voicing:	SA Unison
Accomp:	Piano
Text:	Secular - Christmas - Robert Lee Wolff
Range:	c4-f5
Difficulty:	Med Easy

Style: Rhythmic in a brisk tempo. The work is basically in strophic form with refrain. An interesting and exciting piano accompaniment complements the text painting in the vocal line. Frequent use of short sequential phrases.

Comments: An interesting and accessible work for girls' chorus. Excellent material for a Christmas and/or winter concert.

Publisher:	E.C. Schirmer ECS 4289
Usage:	Secular concert - Christmas

Date: 1986
Level: H.S. - Jr. High

345

Composer: Thompson, Randall
Title: Velvet Shoes
Voicing: SA
Accomp: Piano
Text: Secular - Elinor Wylie
Range: c4-e5, c4-d5
Difficulty: Easy

Style: In ABA form with a short coda, this work is unison throughout except
                 for the eight-bar concluding statement. Traditional harmonies. The
                 piano accompaniment announces each new vocal section with a
                 recurring fanfare. The vocal line is diatonic and almost entirely
                 conjunct.

Comments: This piece is now a classic for young women's voices. Excellent for
                 developing good unison singing, intonation and smooth vocal line.
                 Good material for beginning a new year with a girl's chorus.

Publisher: E.C. Schirmer 2526
Usage: Secular concert
Date: 1960
Level: Junior High - H.S.

346

Composer: Thompson, Randall
Title: My Master hath a Garden
Voicing: SA
Accomp: Piano
Text: Sacred
Range: eb4-eb5, Bb3-Bb4
Difficulty: Easy

Style: This is essentially a strophic song with a short coda. The harmonies are
                 traditional. Rhythmic movement is in quarter and eighth notes, and the
                 voice lines are melodic.

Comments: The work is a simple but tuneful octavo useful for developing phrasing and line in a young girls' chorus. There are no rhythmic or harmonic problems.

Publisher: E.C. Schirmer
Usage: Sacred concert - anthem
Date: 1989
Level: H.S.

347

Composer: Vaughan Williams, Ralph
Title: Sigh No More, Ladies
Voicing: SSA
Accomp: Piano
Text: Secular - Shakespeare
Range: e4-a5, c4-e5, b3-f#5
Difficulty: MED

Style: A rhythmic piece with relatively traditional harmonies and mild dissonances. The form is strophic with chorus and coda. The chorus is homophonic, but the verses set the alto line as solo or soli against paired duets in the soprano.

Comments: A delightful work for a strong girls' chorus. The alto range is a little wide for high school singers. Not an easy piece but well worth the effort.

Publisher: Oxford University Press 54.143
Usage: Secular concert
Date: 1931
Level: H.S. - college

348

Composer: Vaughan Williams, Ralph
Title: The Cloud-Capp'd Towers from THREE SHAKESPEARE SONGS
Voicing: SSAA
Accomp: a cappella
Text: Secular - Shakespeare
Range: a4-a5, c3-e5, f3-c5
Difficulty: Med Dif

Style:	Basically homophonic. Frequent use of chromaticism and shifting tonal centers. Begins in a slow, sustained manner followed by a quicker, more lively section before returning to the opening tempo.
Comments:	A good work for treble voices. Much use of slow, legato lines.
Publisher:	Oxford University Press W17
Usage:	Secular concert
Date:	1956
Level:	H.S.

349

Composer:	Vehar, Persis
Title:	Spring Things
Voicing:	SSA
Accomp:	Piano
Text:	Secular-1)The Voice of the Turtle, Song of Solomon 2)Sweet Lovers, Shakespeare 3)Flower Garden, Heine
Range:	eb4-g5, Bb3-g5, g4-d5
Difficulty:	MED

Style:	Tonal but dissonant with extensive use of tone clusters. All three of these short pieces move at a brisk tempo and are quite rhythmic. A mixture of contrapuntal and homophonic textures. The melodic line is often fragmented and passed between voices.
Comments:	Good program material. This is an intriguing set and would be useful in introducing the choir to sharp dissonances.
Publisher:	Shawnee Press, Inc. B-459
Duration:	3:05
Usage:	Secular concert
Date:	1980
Level:	H.S.

350

Composer:	Washburn, Robert
Title:	Scherzo for Spring
Voicing:	SSA
Accomp:	Piano and Flute or clarinet
Text:	Secular - Spring, the sweet spring, is the year's pleasant king
Range:	Bb3-ab5, ab3-a4

Difficulty:	Easy
Style:	Lively, joyful setting in a fast triple meter. Imitative bird calls appear in the 1st soprano part. Tonal; homophonic. Basically a strophic setting with minor variations and key changes.
Comments:	A delightful and accessible work for a h.s. women's chorus.
Publisher:	Oxford University Press 95.400
Usage:	Secular concert - Spring
Date:	1962
Level:	H.S.

351

Composer:	Fissinger, Edwin
Title:	The Tabernacle of God Is with Men
Voicing:	TTBB
Accomp:	a cappella
Text:	Sacred - from Revelation
Range:	d3-a4, d3-e3,a2-c#4, g2-b3
Difficulty:	Med Diff

Style: A powerful work for men's voices. Quite dissonant, but most dissonances are approached by step. Highly rhythmic with generous use of syncopation and triplet figures. Utilizes wide and rapidly changing dynamic palette. A mixture of homophonic and contrapuntal textures.

Comments: An excellent and challenging work for a good boys' chorus. The piece is written well and sounds well with the male chorus.

Publisher:	Jenson Publications, Inc. 411-20051
Usage:	Sacred-secular concert
Date:	1982
Level:	H.S.

352

Composer:	Hageman, Philip
Title:	Four Songs from Twelfth Night
Voicing:	TTBB
Accomp:	Piano
Text:	Secular-Shakespeare 1) O Mistress Mine 2) Come Away, Death 3) I am Gone, Sir 4) The Rain It Raineth
Range:	a2-a4, a2-f4, a2-eb4, eb2-c#4
Difficulty:	Diff

Style: The first selection alternates between a homophonic A section with close jazz harmonies and a recurring unison B section. The tempo also alternates between a very brisk A section (half note=160) and a much more leisurely B section (half note=69). No 2 is quite dissonant and employs some twelve tone techniques; however, the dissonances are approached by step. No. 3 is a rhythmic four-part canon. No. 4 is sectional, opening with an extended duet; frequently changing meters and tempi.

Comments: Not for the faint hearted; this is challenging material for the high school male chorus. However, the voice parts are well within the singers' ranges. For a strong boys' chorus this would be excellent material.

Publisher: Oxford University Press 95.111
Duration: 10:00
Usage: Secular Concert
Date: 1987
Level: H.S. - College

353

Composer: Harper, John
Title: Psalm 150
Voicing: SA/TB
Accomp: Organ
Text: Sacred - Psalm 150 - Praise God in his holy place, praise him in his mighty heavens...
Range: a4-e5, d4-e5
Difficulty: Easy

Style: The melodic writing is angular and restricted in range. Minor dissonances occur through passing and added tones. Most of the writing is unison with two parts used to accentuate text painting at the words "praise him with resounding cymbals." The organ accompaniment complements the vocal writing. The piece is rhythmic throughout.

Comments: This work would be an effective introit for a high school or adult choir. A short but powerful piece.

Publisher: Oxford University Press E135
Usage: Sacred concert - General anthem
Date: 1974
Level: H.S. - Junior High

354

Composer: Huddinott, Alun
Title: Lisa Lân (Fair Lisa)
Voicing: TTBB
Accomp: Piano
Text: Secular Welsh Folk Song
Range: eb4-eb5, cb4-eb5, eb3-eb4, Bb2-Bb3
Difficulty: MED

Style:	In each of the three verses, the text is set for two voices in parallel thirds over a humming accompaniment. In the first verse the bass and baritone hum in unison under the tenor voices. In verse two the humming accompaniment is in the two tenor voices over the text in the bass-baritone line; in the final verse the text is in the two middle voices with the outer voices humming an accompaniment. Tertian harmonies. Straightforward rhythmic structure. Triple meter throughout.
Comments:	An excellent piece for a high school boys' chorus. The parts lie comfortably within the ranges of high school voices, and the work will sound well with the male chorus.
Publisher:	Oxford University Press 51.031
Usage:	Secular Concert
Date:	1975
Level:	H.S.

355

Composer:	McElheran, Brock
Title:	Here Comes the Avant-Garde
Voicing:	Mixed - Men or Women
Accomp:	Piano & Percussion with optional electronic tape
Text:	Secular - narration illustrated by nonsense syllables
Range:	
Difficulty:	Med Easy
Style:	A tour de force of avant garde techniques. Narrator explains and chorus demonstrates.
Comments:	A novelty piece that would serve as a good introduction to avant garde music for both the audience and the chorus.
Publisher:	Oxford University Press
Usage:	Secular concert
Date:	1969
Level:	H.S.

356

Composer:	McElheran, Brock
Title:	Funeral March on the Deaths of Heroes
Voicing:	Mixed - Men or Women - Speaking chorus

Accomp:	a cappella
Text:	Names of fallen soldiers
Range:	
Difficulty:	Easy

Style: Avant garde. Repetition of different names simultaneously; builds in intensity then recedes, ending in a unison coda.

Comments: Good introduction to avant garde speech techniques. Would be most effective with a medium to large chorus.

Publisher:	Oxford University Press
Usage:	Secular concert
Date:	1969
Level:	H.S.

357

Composer:	Nelson, Ron
Title:	Choral Fanfare for Christmas
Voicing:	TTBB or SATB (some divisi)
Accomp:	3 trumpets, 3 trombones and tuba
Text:	Sacred
Range:	d4-f5, Bb3-c5, f3-e4, Bb2-c4
Difficulty:	MED

Style: A fanfare work characterized by driving rhythms. Meter alternates between 3/4 and 4/4. Extensive use of major chords. Both homophonic and contrapuntal textures are utilized.

Comments: A good, short piece effective as an opener on a Christmas concert. Provides a variety of timbres for the typical concert.

Publisher:	Boosey & Hawkes, Inc.
Usage:	Sacred - secular concert - Christmas
Date:	1960
Level:	H.S.

358

Composer:	Persichetti, Vincent
Title:	Nouns to Nouns
Voicing:	SA/TB
Accomp:	Piano

TTBB

Text:	Secular - e.e. cummings
Range:	e4-f5, b3-b4
Difficulty:	MED

Style: In a lively tempo this piece is rhythmic with frequent use of syncopation. The texture alternates between homophonic and contrapuntal styles. Mildly dissonant vocal parts with greater dissonance in the accompaniment.

Comments: A delightful setting of this e.e. cummings text. Good material for either two-part girls' or boys' chorus.

Publisher:	Elkan-Vogel, Inc. 362-01223
Usage:	Secular concert
Date:	1966
Level:	H.S.

359

Composer:	Pierce, Brent
Title:	My Love Has Gone
Voicing:	SA / TB
Accomp:	Piano
Text:	Secular
Range:	d4-e5, g3-Bb4
Difficulty:	Easy

Style: Contrapuntal throughout. Pierce uses some interesting text painting through his rhythms and dynamics. Although the rhythmic construction in the work is not complex, it intensifies to heighten climactic sections. Mildly dissonant. The accompaniment imitates ringing bells throughout the work.

Comments: This work is best suited for girls' voices. The range of the alto line is too low for tenors and young basses. This is an interesting piece for girls' chorus and would be useful in developing light, sensitive singing.

Publisher:	Plymouth Music Co., Inc. BP - 505
Usage:	Secular concert
Date:	1981
Level:	H.S.

360

Composer:	Pierce, Brent
Title:	Dance of the One-Legged Sailor
Voicing:	SA / TB
Accomp:	Piano
Text:	Secular
Range:	c4-g5, g3-b4
Difficulty:	Med Easy

Style: As the title might indicate, the piece is set in mixed meter, alternating between 6/8, 3/4 and 5/8 time. The tempo is brisk with the dotted quarter=104. The texture is a mixture of homophonic and contrapuntal styles. There is generous use of open fifths and parallel octaves in the accompaniment. Mildly dissonant, mostly in the accompaniment part.

Comments: A rhythmically interesting and fun piece. Good material for a boys' chorus.

Publisher:	Plymouth Music Co., Inc. BP.502
Usage:	Secular concert
Date:	1981
Level:	H.S.

361

Composer:	Pierce, Brent
Title:	Gloria in Excelsis Deo
Voicing:	SA / TB
Accomp:	Piano
Text:	Sacred
Range:	c4-f5, c4-e5
Difficulty:	Med Easy

Style: The texture of this piece is primarily contrapuntal punctuated by short homophonic statements. Mildly dissonant. In 6/8 time the work is rhythmically interesting but presents no particular difficulties. Melodic movement is principally conjunct.

Comments: An interesting two-part work, well suited to either an intermediate level girls' or boys' chorus.

Publisher:	Plymouth Music Co., Inc. BP.503
Usage:	Sacred - secular concert
Date:	1981
Level:	H.S.

362

Composer:	Pierce, Brent
Title:	Come and Follow Me
Voicing:	SA / TB
Accomp:	Piano
Text:	Secular - Come and follow me across the sea. Come and be my love...
Range:	g3-d5, g3-d5
Difficulty:	Easy

Style: With the exception of a six-bar phrase, this piece is written entirely as a two-part canon. The vocal lines are conjunct. The accompaniment is somewhat dissonant. Basic rhythmic movement is by eighth notes in duple meter.

Comments: This would be good material for a young chorus. Although the piece is indicated for SA or TB, the voicing works best for girls.

Publisher:	Plymouth Music Co., Inc. BP.501
Usage:	Secular concert
Date:	1981
Level:	H.S. - Junior High

363

Composer:	Schickele, Peter
Title:	Captain Fate from THREE PIRATE SONGS
Voicing:	TB
Accomp:	Piano
Text:	Secular - Peter Schickele
Range:	f3-e4, Bb2-c4
Difficulty:	Med Easy

Style: This is a strophic song with a brief introduction and coda. The accompaniment is repetitive, effectively creating images of a rolling sea. The two-voice vocal part is homophonic throughout, utilizing quartal harmonies. The meter is 6/8 at a moderate tempo although the sixteenth-note and sixteenth-note triplet figures in the accompaniment give momentum to the piece. The vocal lines are primarily conjunct and easily singable.

Comments: An easy but effective work for boys' chorus. A rousing ending piece for a concert group.

Publisher: Elkan-Vogel, Inc. 362-03296

Duration: 3:00
Usage: Secular concert
Date: 1980
Level: H.S. - College

364

Composer: Schickele, Peter
Title: We Have Crossed the Equator Again from THREE PIRATE SONGS
Voicing: TTBB
Accomp: Piano
Text: Secular - Peter Schickele
Range: d3-a4, g2-e4
Difficulty: MED

Style: The work opens with a short, slow introduction before moving into the
                 rhythmic, rapidly moving central section. The meter alternates between
                 duple and triple; rhythmic complexity is created between the vocal parts
                 and the accompaniment through the extensive use of hemiola.
                 Harmonies are characterized by frequent use of second inversion chords
                 and the pentatonic scale. Vocal lines are complemented by the driving
                 rhythms in the piano accompaniment.

Comments: The harmonies in this work are quite accessible and punctuated by
                 frequent unison passages. A fun and exciting selection for a boys'
                 chorus. Highly recommended.

Publisher: Elkan-Vogel, Inc. 362-03298
Duration: 5:00
Usage: Secular concert
Date: 1980
Level: H.S. - College

365

Composer: Stevens, Halsey
Title: All this Night Shrill Chanticleer
Voicing: TBB
Accomp: a cappella
Text: Secular - All this night shrill chanticleer, day's proclaiming trumpeter...
Range: e3-a4, d3-e4, f2-d4
Difficulty: Med Easy

Style: Homophonic. Harmony is characterized by frequent movement in parallel thirds and the use of open 4ths and 5ths. Shifting meters and rhythmic accents within a brisk tempo [half note=96]. The work encompasses a broad dynamic range.

Comments: A good introduction to some 20th-century sonorities for the male choir. Will sound well with the male chorus.

Publisher: Peer-Southern 02-12027-014
Duration: 2:40
Usage: Christmas
Date: 1954
Level: H.S. - College

                                366

Composer: Stravinsky, Igor
Title: Four Russian Peasant Songs *
Voicing: SSAA or TTBB solos in each voice part
Accomp: a cappella
Text: Secular English and Russian texts
Range: e4-f5, e4-e5, b3-d4, a3-a4
Difficulty: Med Dif

Style: Frequently changing meters and varied rhythmic effects. Extensive unison and two-part writing. Melodic lines lie within restricted ranges. Work is typical of early Stravinsky; close harmony, frequent 2nds, highly rhythmic and somewhat repetitive.

Comments: Good introduction to Stravinsky. Set may be performed in its entirety or individual pieces may be performed separately.

Publisher: Edward B. Marks Music Corp. MC27
Duration: 4:
Usage: Secular concert
Date: 1917
Level: H.S.

                                367

Composer: Vaughan Williams, Ralph
Title: Drinking Song - Back and Side Go Bare
Voicing: TTBB
Accomp: Piano

Text:	Secular - Back and side go bare, both foot and hand go cold; but belly, God send thee good ale ...
Range:	c3-a4, c3-f4, g2-d4, g2-d4
Difficulty:	MED
Style:	Fast in duple meter; rhythmically, quite straightforward. The piece is modal with conjunct writing in the voice parts. It is primarily set for two voice parts with occasional introduction of three- and four-part textures. Rhythmic movement is in quarter- and eighth-note patterns. Piano accompaniment is not particularly difficult but adds zest to the work.
Comments:	A fun piece for male chorus. Readily accessible to high school singers and a good show piece for the boys' chorus.
Publisher:	Oxford University Press 51.028
Duration:	1:00
Usage:	Secular concert
Date:	1931
Level:	H.S. - College

Music Publishers

AB Carl Gehrman Musikforlag (Walton Music Corp.)

Abingdon Press (Hope)

Agape (Hope)

Alexander Broude, Inc. (Tetra)

Alfred Music
16380 Roscoe Blvd
Van Nuys, CA 91410-0003

Anderson Associates
1739 S. Douglas Rd. Suite F
Anaheim, CA 92806

Arista Music Co.
Box 1596
Brooklyn NY 11201

Associated Music Pub. (G. Schirmer/Hal Leonard)

Augsburg Publishing House
426 S. Fifth Street
Minneapolis, MN 55415

Beckenhorst Press, Inc.
3821 N. High
Columbus, Ohio 43214

Belwin Mills Publishing Corp. (CPP/Belwin)

Boosey & Hawkes
52 Cooper Square
New York, N.Y. 10003

Bourne Co.
5 West 37th St.
New York, N.Y. 10018

Broude Bros., Ltd.
141 White Oaks Rd.
Williamstown, MA 01267

Canyon Press, Inc. (E.C. Kirby Ltd.)

Carl Fischer, Inc.
56-62 Cooper Square
New York, NY 10003

Chanteclair Music (Gordon V. Thompson Ltd.)

Concordia Publishing House
3558 South Jefferson Ave.
St. Louis, MO 63118

Continuo Music Press Inc. (Alexander Broude)

CPP/Belwin
15800 N.W. 48th Ave.
Miami, FL 33014

Curtis House of Music (Kjos)

Curtis Music Press (Kjos)

Durand & Cie (Theodore Presser)

E.C. Schirmer Music Co.
138 Ipswich St.
Boston, MA 02215

E.C. Kirby, Ltd. (Hal Leonard)

Editions Salabert (G. Schirmer/Hal Leonard)

Edward B. Marks (Hal Leonard)

Elkan-Vogel, Inc. (Theodore Presser)

European American Music
P.O. Box 850
Valley Forge, PA 19482

Fostco Music Press (Mark Foster Music Co.)

Franco Columbo Inc. (Belwin)

G. Schirmer, Inc. (G. Schirmer/Hal Leonard)

G. Schirmer/Hal Leonard Publishing Co.
7777 W. Bluemound
Milwaukee, WI 53213

G.I.A. Publications, Inc.
7404 S. Mason
Chicago, IL 60638
Galaxy Music Co. (E.C. Schirmer)

Galleria Press
170 N.E. 33rd St.
Ft. Lauderdale, FL 33334

Gordon V. Thompson Ltd.
29 Birch Ave.
Toronto, Ontario, Canada

Greenwood Press (World)

Hal Leonard Publishing Co.
7777 W. Bluemound
Milwaukee, WI 53213

Harold Flammer Inc.
1 Waring Dr.
Delaware Water Gap, PA 18327

Helios Music Edition (Mark Foster)

Hinshaw Music Inc.
P.O. Box 478
Chapel Hill, NC 27514

Hope Publishing Co.
360 S. Main Place
Carol Stream, IL 60187

Ione Press, Inc. (E.C. Schirmer)

J. Christopher Music Co. (Theodore Presser)

J. Curwen & Sons Ltd. (G. Schirmer)

Jenson Publications (Hal Leonard)

Lorenz Publishing Co.
501 East 3rd St.
Dayton, OH 45401

John Sheppard Music Press (Boonin)

Joseph Boonin, Inc. (European American Music)

Lawson-Gould (Alfred)

Mark Foster Music Co.
Box 4012
Champaign, IL 61820

Mercury Music Corp. (Theodore Presser)

Merion Music, Inc. (Theodore Presser)

Music Sales, Corp.
5 Bellvale Rd.
Chester, N.Y. 10918

National Music Publishers (Anderson Associates)

Neil A. Kjos
4382 Jutland Dr.
San Diego, CA 92117

Novello & Co., Ltd. (Theodore Presser)

Oxford University Press
200 Madison Ave.
New York, NY 10019

Paul A. Schmitt Music Co. (Belwin)

Peer International Corp. (Theodore Presser)

Peer-Southern (Theodore Presser)

Plymouth Music Co., Inc.
170 N.E. 33rd St.
Ft. Lauderdale, FL 33334

Roger Dean Publishing Co. (Lorenz)

Rongwen Music, Inc. (Broude Brothers)

Sacred Music Press (Lorenz)

Schott & Co. (European American)

Shawnee Press, Inc.
1 Waring Dr.
Delaware Water Gap, PA 18327

Stainer & Bell (Galaxy Music Co.)

Standard Music Publishing, Inc.
P.O. Box 1043
Turnersville, NJ 08012
Summy-Birchard Pub. Co. (Warner Bros.)

Tetra Music Corp. (Plymouth)

Theodore Presser Co.
Presser Place
Bryn Mawr, PA 19010

W-7 Music Corp. (Hal Leonard)

Walton Music Corp. (Plymouth)

Warner Bros. Publications Inc.
265 Secaucus Rd.
Secaucus, N.J. 07096-2037

Western International Music
3707 65th Ave.
Greely, CO 80634-9626

Westwood Press, Inc. (World Library)

Wilhelm Hansen (Music Sales)

Word Music Inc.
5221 N. O'Connor Blvd., Suite 100
Irving, TX 75039

World Library Publications, Inc.
3815 N. Willow Rd.
Schiller PK, IL 60176

Composer Index

Adams, Leslie 1
Adler, Samuel 1
Ahrold, Frank 2, 154
Archibeque, Charlene 2
Arnatt, Ronald 3

Baksa, Robert 4, 154, 155
Barber, Samuel 5, 6
Bardos, Lajos 155
Bartók, Belá 7
Bassett, Leslie 7
Bavicchi, John 8
Beadell, Robert 8
Beck, John Ness 9, 10
Bell, Robert Hunter 156
Benjamin, Thomas 10, 110
Berger, Jean 11-14
Biggs, John 14
Binkerd, Gordon 15
Bliss, Arthur 15
Boyajian, Gloria 110
Boyd, Jack 16
Bright, Houston 16, 111
Britten, Benjamin 17, 18, 111, 156
Butler, Eugene 19, 112, 157

Carter, John 112
Casals, Pablo 113, 157, 158
Chavez, Carlos 20
Christopherson, Dorothy 145
Clark, Rogie 20
Clausen, René 21, 113
Clothier, Louitha 21
Copland, Aaron 22, 114
Crocker, Emily 145, 158

Dello Joio, Norman 23, 24
Diemer, Emma Lou 25
Dietterich, Philip R. 146
Distler, Hugo 25-28, 146-148, 159, 160
Donahue, Robert 28
Donato, Anthony 160
Durufle, Maurice 29, 161
Duson, Dede 30, 161, 162

Effinger, Cecil 31-33

Felciano, Richard 34, 114, 162, 163
Ferris, William 115
Fetler, Paul 35, 36, 116
Fine, Irving 117
Fink, Michael 36, 37
Fissinger, Edwin 38, 117-120, 190
Forsyth, Malcolm 164
Frackenpohl, Arthur 38, 39, 164
Fritschel, James 120, 121

Gardner, John 39
Goemanne, Noel 40
Gooch, Warren P. 40
Grantham, Donald 41
Gustafson, Dwight 41

Hageman, Philip 42, 148, 190
Harper, John 165, 191
Harris, Robert A. 43, 122, 166
Haufrecht, Herbert 43
Healey, Derek 44
Hemberg, Eskil 45
Henderson, Ruth Watson 166, 167
Hennagin, Michael 122, 167
Hillert, Richard 123
Hindemith, Paul 45
Holland, Wilfrid 168, 169
Holst, Gustav T. 169
Hopson, Hal H. 46
Hovhaness, Alan 170
Hovland, Egil 123, 170
Huddinott, Alun 191
Hurd, David 47
Hutcheson, Jere 47

Ives, Charles 48, 124

Jackson, Hanley 48-50
Jennings, Kenneth 50, 51
Jergenson, Dale 52
Johanson, Sven-Eric 52, 53

Kodaly, Zoltan 171, 172
Kraehenbuehl, David 125

Krenek, Ernst 172
Kreutz, Robert E. 53, 54

Lamb, Gordon H. 54
Larsen, Libby 55, 125
Larsson, Lars-Erik 55
Leavitt, John 149
Lekberg, Sven 56, 173
Lovelock, William 56, 126
Luboff, Norman 127

MacGillivray, Allister 173
Manz, Paul O. 57
Marshall, Jane 174
Mathew, David 127
Mathias, William 57, 128
Maw, Nicholas 58, 59
McCray, James 59-61
McElheran, Brock 174, 175, 192
McKay, David P. 61
Mechem, Kirke 62, 128, 175-177
Medema, Ken 63
Mellnas, Arne 177
Mennin, Peter 63
Moe, Daniel 64-67, 129
Mollicone, Henry 67, 68
Monhardt, Maurice 68

Nagel, Robert 69
Nelhybel, Vaclav 178
Nelson, Ron 69, 70, 193
Nelson, Ronald A. 149
Nickson, John A. 70
Nin-Culmell, Joaquin 130
Nystedt, Knut 71, 130-133

Page, Robert 134, 178
Papale, Henry 150
Parker, Alice 71
Pasquet, Jean 150
Paul, David 72
Peeters, Flor 72
Persichetti, Vincent 73, 134, 179,
        193
Petzold, Johannes 74
Pfautsch, Lloyd 74-77
Pierce, Brent 77, 78, 135, 179-181,
        194, 195, 197
Piket, Frederick 78
Pinkham, Daniel 79, 80, 181
Poorman, Sonja 135

Poulenc, Francis 81, 136
Powell, Robert 81

Rabe, Folke 82
Rickard, Jeffrey H. 136
Riegger, Wallingford 137
Roff, Joseph 151
Rorem, Ned 82, 83
Ross, M. Keith 84
Rutter, John 84-86, 137, 138, 182,
        183

Sateren, Leland B. 183
Schickele, Peter 87, 197, 198
Schuman, William 87-90, 151
Seiber, Mátyás 90
Slater, Richard W. 91
Smith, Robert Edward 91
Smith, Russell 184
Spencer, Williametta 92, 93, 139
Steinmetz, John 93
Stevens, Halsey 94, 95, 140, 141,
        198
Stravinsky, Igor 184, 199
Susa, Conrad 95, 96

Tate, Phyllis 97, 185
Thompson, Randall 97-102, 141,
        185, 186
Thybo, Leif 103
Toch, Ernst 103
Track, Gerhard 142
Trubitt, Allen R. 104

Vaughan Williams, Ralph 104, 142,
        143, 187, 199
Vehar, Persis 188
Vick, Lloyd 143

Walter, Samuel 105
Walton, William 105
Washburn, Robert 106, 107, 188
Welin, Karl-Erik 107
Wetzler, Robert 108
White, Louise L. 108
Whitecotton, Shirley 152
Willcocks, David (arr.) 144
Wood, Dale 152

Zaimont, Judith Lang 144

Title Index

Aglepta 177
Aleatory Psalm * 54
All Day I Hear 35
All That Hath Life and Breath Praise Ye the Lord 113
All this Night Shrill Chanticleer 198
Alleluia 102
American Indian Songs 51
And Back Again 162
. . . And Sparrows Everywhere 125
Anthony O Daly #2 from REINCARNATIONS 6
Arbolucu, te sequeste * 20
Arise, Shine, for Thy Light has Come 51
Arise, Shine, For Thy Light Is Come 117
As the Deer Crieth 146
Ascribe Unto the Lord * 91
At the Round Earth's Imagined Corners 139
August Noon 16
Awake, My Soul * 149

A Babe is Born 129
Barbara Allen 144
Basket #3 of FOUR PASTORALES 32
Be Still 120
Bees 103
The Bells 2
The Best of Rooms 100
The Birds 96
Birds are Never Soaring Too High 55
Blow, Blow, Thou Winter Wind 137
By the Springs of Water 31
By the Waters of Babylon 119

Canco a la Verge (Hymn to the Virgin) 158
Canticle of Praise 10
Canticle: The Hungry Angels 122
Captain Fate from THREE PIRATE SONGS 197
A Carol for New Year's Day 79
Caution #3 from FOUR ROUNDS ON FAMOUS WORDS 151
A Child Said 60
A Child's Ghetto 50
Choose Something Like a Star from FROSTIANA 99
Choral Fanfare for Christmas 69, 193
A Choral Miscellany * 150
Chorus 93
A Christmas Carol 24
Circus Band 124

Clap Your Hands 40
Clap Your Hands * 119
A Clear Midnight   from CELEBRATIONS 134
The Cloud-Capp'd Towers from THREE SHAKESPEARE SONGS 187
Collect 7
Come and Follow Me 181, 197
Come Away, Death 142
Come Follow Me 149
Come Sing Madrigals * 61
Come, Make a Joyful Sound 46
Come, Spirit Divine 27
Come, Thou Fount of Every Blessing 76
Concord from CHORAL DANCES FROM GLORIANA 18
The Coolin #3 from REINCARNATIONS 6
Cosmic Festival from TWO PUBLIC PIECES 162
Country Girls from CHORAL DANCES FROM GLORIANA 156
Create in Me a Clean Heart 150
Crossing the Han River 63
The Cynic 176

Dance of the One-Legged Sailor 180, 195
Dancing Song 171
Dan-U-EL 128
De Gustibus 148
Death Carol from WHEN LILACS LAST IN THE DOORYARD 126
Dispute Among Divines - #4 from BENJAMIN FRANKLIN 43
Drinking Song - Back and Side Go Bare 199

Easter Carol * 48
E'en So, Lord Jesus, Quickly Come 57
Eldorado 42
The Elusive Quest 30
Engraved on the Collar of a Dog, which I gave to His Royal Highness 97
The Eyes of All Hope in Thee, O Lord 34
The Eyes of All Wait Upon Thee 11

Fain Would I Change That Note 104
Fall Softly, Snow * 129
Fancies I 52
Fancies II 53
A Farewell 175
For God So Loved the World 148
For the Beauty of the Earth 183
Four Carols for a Holy Night 56
Four Chinese Poems 107
Four Russian Peasant Songs * 184, 199
Four Songs from Twelfth Night   190
The Frog in the Well 185
Full Fadom Five Thy Father Lies (second setting) 37
Funeral March on the Deaths of Heroes 175, 192

Geographical Fugue 103
Gloria 136
Gloria in Excelsis Deo 180, 195
Gloria Patri 127
Glory to God in the Highest 101
Go and Tell John 76
Go, Lovely Rose 95
God Has Gone Up with a Shout! Alleluia! 123
God Rest Ye Merry, Gentlemen 23

The Happy Shore 98
Have You Seen the White Lily Grow? #2 from THE HOUR GLASS 117
Health #2 from FOUR ROUNDS ON FAMOUS WORDS 90
The Heavenly Aeroplane 182
Here Comes the Avant-Garde 174, 192
Hogamus, Higamus * 164
The Holy Infant's Lullaby 24
Holy Valley 154
Hosanna #2 from JAZZ FRAGMENTS 78
Hosanna * 36
Hosanna to the Son of David 1, 64
How Glorious Your Name, O Lord 53
How Still He Rests 77
Hungarian Folksongs 94
Hunting Song 157
A Hymn for Advent 9
A Hymn to the Virgin 111
Hymn to Vena from CHORAL HYMNS FROM THE RIG VEDA 169

I Hear America Singing 75
I Saw a Stable - #2 of CAROLS TO PLAY AND SING 71
I to the Hills Lift Up Mine Eyes 13
I Will be as the Dew * 133
I Will Give Thanks to the Lord 61
I Will Praise Thee, O Lord 132
Identity 127
Ideo gloria in excelsis Deo * 125
If you Receive My Words * 132
If You Your Lips Would Keep from Slips * 31
In Excelsis Gloria! 72
In Paradisum 172
In Peace and Joy 121
In the Beginning of Creation 79
In the Summer * 155
In the World there Is Pain 28
In Unison 161
It Was a Lover and his Lass 57, 138

Jig from FIVE IRISH SONGS 58
Jubilate Deo 60

Kyrie   from A THANKSGIVING MASS   133

The Lamb   166
Lament for a Lost Child   47
The Lament of Job   52
Lamentations of Jeremiah   131
The Last Invocation   from CAROLS OF DEATH   88
The Last Invocation *   112
The Last Words of David   102
Late Have I Loved Thee   112
Laudate Dominum   110, 170
Laughing Song   62, 108
Let All the World in Every Corner Sing   173
Let Down the Bars, O Death   5
Let the People Praise Thee   68
Let the People Praise Thee, O God   128
Let the Whole Creation Cry Glory *   110
Let Your Eye be to the Lord   67
Lied vom Winde   160
Lift Up Your Heads   174
Lift Up Your Heads, Ye Mighty Gates   159
The Light of Stars   99
The Lighthearted Lovers   62
Like as the Culver on the Bared Bough   140
Lisa Lân (Fair Lisa)   191
Listen to Me *   71
Lo! How a Rose E'er Blooming   26
Lob auf die Musik   27
The Lord Has a Child   87
Lord of the Winds   21
Lord, Keep us Steadfast   147
Love Came Down at Christmas   3
Lovers Love the Spring   39
Lullaby from A CHRISTMAS CELEBRATION   67

Madman   16
Make a Joyful Noise   116
Make Haste, O God   118
Make We Joy   120
Maria Walks Amid the Thorn   147
Memory, hither come   181
The Message #2 from THE WINGED JOY   177
Modern Music   115
More Than Raiment *   74
Moses   63
Music Here   19
Musicks Empire from TRIPTYCH   77
My Heart Dances   121
My Heart is Ready   145
My Love Has Gone   179, 194
My Master hath a Garden   186

Mystic Trumpeter 92

Never Doubt I Love 38
A New Year Carol 168
Night Hymn * 19
The Night Will Never Stay 54
Nigra Sum 157
No Mark #1 from FOUR PASTORALES 33
Noon #2 from FOUR PASTORALES 33
Nothing is Here for Tears 143
The Not-Yet Flower (A Crisis of Growth) from TWO PUBLIC PIECES 163
Nouns to Nouns 179, 193
Now Welcome Summer 107
Numbers in a Row 72

O Clap Your Hands 85
O Come, O Come Emmanuel 163
O Crux 130
O King Enthroned on High * 44
O Lady Moon * 170
O Love That Triumphs Over Loss 146
O My Luve's Like a Red, Red Rose 93
O Praise Ye the Lord 152
O Sacrum Convivium 156
O Sweet Jesu 15
O Vos Omnes 113
Of Mirth and Merriment 12
Oh, How Can I Keep from Singing? 43
On Christmas Day 28
One May Morning 2
Open Thou Mine Eyes 138
Outdoor Three 183

The Paper Reeds by the Brooks from THE PEACEABLE KINGDOM 101
Passages 59
Piping Anne and Husky Paul 80
Popular Song #3 of FIVE IRISH SONGS * 59
Praise to the Lord, the Almighty 25
Praise Ye the Lord 86
A Prayer of Supplication 46
Pretty Polly (No. 2 of TWO BALLADS) 95
The Promise of Living from THE TENDER LAND 114
Proverb 73
Proverbs #3 from AIRS AND ROUNDS 14
Psalm 117 * 38
Psalm 117: O Praise the Lord, All Ye Nations 141
Psalm 150 165, 191
Psalm Concertato Pt.I * 65
Psalm Concertato Pt.II * 64
Psalm Concertato Pt.III * 65
Psalm XXI 49

Quem vidistis pastores from THREE CHRISTMAS MOTETS 134, 178

Red Rosey Bush (No. 1 of TWO BALLADS) 96
Rejoice, Alleluia 145
Riddle Song 86
The Road not Taken   from FROSTIANA 100
Rocking * 34
Rondes 82
A Rose Touched by the Sun's Warm Rays 11
A Rustic Song 169

St. Gregory's Day 172
Saint Teresa's Book Mark 108
Saul 123
Scherzo for Spring 188
Sea Charm 78
Seeds Grow to Plants 84
Send Forth, O God, Thy Light and Truth 68
Set Me As A Seal from A NEW CREATION 21
The Sheepheards Song 80
She's Like a Swallow 55
Sigh No More, Ladies 187
Sigh No More, Ladies * 9
Signposts 45
Since all is Passing #3 of SIX CHANSONS 45
Sing and Dance 10
Sing Me the Universal from CELEBRATIONS 73
Sing to God 142
Sing Unto God 116
Sing We and Dance 135
Sing with Joy, Glad Voices Lift 26
Six Afro-American Carols 20
Six Alleluia Canons 47
The Sixty-Seventh Psalm 124
Solstice 185
Some One 1
Song for Evening 160
Song for the Mira 173
Songs of Late Summer 155
A Spotless Rose 3
Spring Things 188
The Stars are with the Voyager 111
Stomp Your Foot   from THE TENDER LAND 22
Storm from THROUGH THE EYES OF CHILDREN 167
Stranger, Share Our Fire * 66
The Straw Guy 171
Sung for the Passing of a Beautiful Woman from SONGS FROM THE PAIUTE 140
Sunny Airs and Sober (A Book of Madrigals) 144
Sweet Day, So Cool 15
Sweet Sunny 23

The Tabernacle of God Is with Men 190
Take, Oh Take Those Lips Away 70
Tantum ergo   from QUATRE MOTETS 29
Tenebrae factae sunt 81
That's the Idea of Freedom from THE SECOND HURRICANE 22
There is a Garden in Her Face 13
There is one Body 44
This Is My Letter to the World from SEVEN CHORAL SETTINGS 41
Thou Hidden Love of God * 105
Three American Choruses 8
Three Choruses from e.e. cummings 87
Three Emily Dickinson Songs 167
Three Hungarian Folk Songs 7
Three Hungarian Folk-songs 90
Three Madrigals 25
Three Motets 83
Three Prayers 83
Three Precious Gifts 154
Three Songs of Parting * 41
Three Songs on the Shortness of Life * 104
Three Traditional Cuban Songs 130
Three Zulu Songs 164
Thrift #2 of FOUR ROUNDS ON FAMOUS WORDS 89
Thy Truth is Great 70
Time and Concord from CHORAL DANCES FROM GLORIANA 17
Time from CHORAL DANCES FROM GLORIANA 17
Timor et tremor 136
To a Mosquito * 151
To All, to Each from CAROLS OF DEATH 88
To Be Sung on the Water 5
To Make a Prairie   from THREE POEMS 12
Tomorrow Shall Be My Dancing Day 39
Tota Pulchra from QUATRE MOTETS 161
Travelog 135
Triptych * 69
Tu es Petrus #3 of QUATRE MOTETS 29
Tubal Cain 152
Two Choral Fanfares 143
Two Motets * 14
Two Songs of Longing 158
Two Worlds 97

The Unknown Region from CAROLS OF DEATH 89

Velvet Shoes 186
Very Long Ago 40
Vignettes of the Plains * 49
Voyager's Song from THREE THOUGHTS FROM THOREAU 106

Walking on the Green Grass 122

Walking So Early 4
We Have Crossed the Equator Again from THREE PIRATE SONGS 198
We Talked as Girls Do from THREE SONGS FROM EMILY DICKINSON * 184
Welcome Yule 118
What Cheer? 105
What Star is This * 82
What Sweeter Music 36, 85
When Love is Kind 178
Where are All Thy Beauties Now 91
Who Can Revoke 137
Who Hath a Right to Sing? from SONGS OF EXPERIENCE 74
Who Is at My Window? 56
Wild Swans 35
Winter 4
Winter from SONGS FROM THE PAIUTE 94
With a Voice of Singing 50
Wood #4 from FOUR PASTORALES 32
Words of St. Peter * 114
Wrestling Jacob 84

The Yak and The Train Dogs (Musical Animal Tales Set II) 166
Ye Were Sometimes Darkness from REQUIEM 141